18^{s}

$99BB$

Dual-Career Couples

A SPECIAL ISSUE OF
PSYCHOLOGY OF WOMEN QUARTERLY

Edited by
Jeff B. Bryson, Ph.D.
and
Rebecca Bryson, Ph.D.

 **HUMAN SCIENCES PRESS**
72 Fifth Avenue   3 Henrietta Street
NEW YORK, NY 10011 ● LONDON, WC2E 8LU

Library of Congress Catalog Number 77-89983
ISBN: 0-87705-371-5
Copyright 1978 by Human Sciences Press

HUMAN SCIENCES PRESS
72 Fifth Avenue
New York, New York 10011

Printed in the United States of America

CONTENTS

VOLUME 3 NUMBER 1　　　　　　　　　　**FALL 1978**

The *Psychology of Women Quarterly* is the official publication of Division 35 of the American Psychological Association. Empirical studies, critical reviews, theoretical articles, and invited book reviews are published in the *Quarterly*. Unusual findings in studies otherwise not warranting a full report may be written as brief reports. The kinds of problems addressed include: psychobiological factors, behavioral studies, role development and change, career choice and training, management variables, education, discrimination, therapeutic processes, and sexuality. These suggestions are not meant to be exhaustive, but rather to guide investigations in the psychology of women.

MANUSCRIPTS must be sent in triplicate to: Professor Georgia Babladelis, Editor, *Psychology of Women Quarterly*, Department of Psychology, California State University, Hayward, California 94542. Blind review procedures are used. Authors are responsible for preserving their anonymity in the pages of their manuscript. Style is according to the APA Publication Manual, 1974 revision. The Publication Manual is available in most departments or libraries or can be purchased from: American Psychological Association, 1200-17th Street, N.W., Washington, D.C. 20036. Authors should seek written permission from the copyright owner (usually the publisher) for the use of tables, illustrations, or extensively quoted material which has previously appeared in another publication. Articles are published in the order in which they are accepted. Provisions for early publication of an accepted article can be made if the author is willing to pay the cost of the extra pages required. No free reprints are available to the author, but reprints may be purchased from the publisher.

SUBSCRIPTIONS are on an academic year basis: $35 per year. Rates for individual professionals and students are available on request from the Business Office. Foreign subscriptions are an additional $4. ADVERTISING and subscription inquiries should be made to Human Sciences Press, 72 Fifth Avenue, New York, New York 10011. (212) 243-6000. Rates are available on request.

OVERSEAS SUBSCRIBERS Human Sciences Press, 3 Henrietta Street, London, WC2E 8LU England.

INDEXED in Sociological Abstracts, Human Resources Abstracts, Psychological Abstracts, Social Sciences Citation Index, Current Contents/Social and Behavioral Sciences, Current Index to Journals in Education (CIJE), Chicorel Abstracts to Reading and Learning Disabilities, Child Development Abstracts and Bibliography, Development and Welfare (India), Human Sexuality Update, Marriage and Family Review, Sage Family Studies Abstracts.

L.C.: 76—12952   ISSN: 0361 6843   PWOQDY 3(1) 1-120 (1978)

EDITORIAL

This special issue on dual-career couples inaugurates Volume 3 of the *Psychology of Women Quarterly*. In previous editorials and elsewhere we have committed ourselves to the idea of periodically bringing together a substantive body of research on one topic in a special issue of the journal. Special issues in progress include the future of work for women, black women, androgyny, therapeutic treatment of women, relationships, child care, biographies of women psychologists, and attention to middle-aged and aging women.

At the meetings of the American Psychological Association in Chicago, 1975, I attended a symposium on dual-career couples. Among the participants were Rebecca and Jeff Bryson and Barbara Wallston. The symposium was well attended, and the lively discussion that took place between audience and participants indicated the high degree of interest in information on dual-career couples. I discussed with Barbara Wallston, whom I knew well from our work in Division 35, the possibility of bringing together information on dual-career couples in a special issue of the *Quarterly*. She convinced me that scholarly work was being done, and we agreed on the appropriateness of inviting a dual-career couple to be guest editors for this special issue. The Brysons agreed to take on the task. In the ensuing two and a half years they probably experienced many misgivings over that decision but they persevered, thus providing me with a personally rewarding working relationship and all of us with an informative and stimulating accomplishment.

Because of wide interest in the information about dual-career couples, our publishers plan to publish this special issue as a separate book also. We thank Norma Fox, Vice-President of Human Sciences Press, for extending the availability of this important work to all interested people.

We hope you find this special issue informative and provocative. To paraphrase Shakespeare (a hazardous if not foolhardy enterprise): there are more ideas 'twixt these covers, dear reader, than our psychology does tell of—yet.

Georgia Babladelis
California State University, Hayward

5

PREFACE

The incidence of dual-career or dual-worker families has been increasing at a consistent pace over the past decade. Currently, nearly half of all married women who live with their husbands are employed. According to data from the U.S. Bureau of Labor Statistics, 55.6% of wives with school-age children and 37.4% of wives with preschoolers were employed in 1977. As wives are increasingly disposed to seek outside employment, or to retain their jobs after marriage, it seems clear that some very major changes and adjustments must be made, both within individual families and in society's attitudes toward dual-career families.

What kinds of changes do people see as necessary? What kinds are occurring? In a broad, general sense, what are the personal and professional effects of dual employment on the husbands and wives in dual-career marriages? This special issue of *Psychology of Women Quarterly* is devoted to papers dealing with the dual-career couple. Included are papers considering job-seeking, domestic responsibility, effects of having children, personal values, and marital adjustment.

For those couples who engage in job-seeking, the difficulties associated with finding two acceptable positions in the same geographical area represent an early source of frustration and, generally, a reminder of some of the kinds of trade-offs that are necessary to sustain a dual-career marriage. In their paper "I Will Follow Him: Myth, Reality, or Forced Choice—Job-Seeking Experiences of Dual-Career Couples," Barbara Wallston, Martha Foster, and Michael Berger examine considerations made by the couple in both real and simulated job-seeking situations. The second paper in the issue, "Anti-Nepotism's Ghost: Attitudes of Administrators Toward Hiring Professional Couples," by Suzanne Pingree, Matilda Butler, William Paisley, and Robert Hawkins, considers the professional couple's job-seeking dilemma from another point of view, examining the extent to which academic administrators hold attitudes that would be prejudicial to the hiring of a couple.

In addition to difficulties associated with job-seeking, the dual-career couple, at some early stage of their relationship, must either explicitly or by default work out a pattern for sharing domestic responsibilities. Donald St. John-Parsons has considered this as well as other issues in his interviews with dual-career couples. In his paper "Continuous Dual-Career Families: A Case Study" he presents data, consistent with other studies, that suggest a disproportionate share of the household responsibilities tends to be assumed by the wife. That egalitarianism is clearly not the norm is also reported by Kathy Weingarten in her paper "The Employment Pattern of Professional Couples and Their Distribution of Involvement in the Family." She does, however, find some minimization of differences in husband/wife participation associated with employment history: Those couples with similar employment histories were more likely to share domestic responsibilities.

There are clearly large individual differences in the amount of household responsibility assumed by the husband. Carolyn Perrucci, Harry Potter, and Deborah Rhoads have examined these in their paper "Determinants of Male Family–Role Performance." They proceed to test three competing hypotheses that have been offered to explain the extent (or lack) of husband participation: socialization-ideology, relative resources, and time availability. Of these, socialization appeared to receive the strongest support, with no support for the time-availability argument.

The St. John-Parsons paper further considers how children affect the role performance of husband and wife. While he found greater efforts at accommodation on the part of the wife, he did not find evidence for an associated tendency for wives to take a lightened professional load to provide time for handling this added responsibility. The considerable role strain and simple lack of available time that are generated by this accommodation are probable reasons for the generally lower job and domestic satisfaction of the wives in dual-career couples with children, reported in the study by Rebecca Bryson, Jeff Bryson, and Marilyn Johnson, entitled "Family Size, Satisfaction, and Productivity."

Two other papers in the issue compare the adjustment of dual-career couples with that of "traditional" couples. Willa Huser and Claude Grant compare couples in terms of personal values in their paper "A Study of Husbands and Wives from Dual-Career and Traditional-Career Families." They found little evidence of differences in values between these two groups, with the exception that the dual-career couples tended to be more inner-directed and flexible. The final paper in this issue, "Wives' Employment Status and Marital Adjustment: Yet Another Look," by Graham Staines, Joseph Pleck, Linda Shepard, and Pamela O'Connor, provides an excellent review of the literature on the general question of employment and marital satisfaction and attempts to isolate the conditions that lead to the frequently reported negative relationship between wives' employment and marital satisfaction. This paper offers an unusually thorough analysis of data from two large national survey samples.

While we served as the co-editors for this special issue, two other people should be recognized for their efforts in seeing that the issue was realized. Barbara Strudler Wallston originated the idea for this special issue and was the person most responsible for selling the idea to the *Quarterly*. She receives our approbation for getting this issue started and our envy for her wisdom and skill in evading the editorial duties. Georgia Babladelis, the editor of *Psychology of Women Quarterly*, was a continual source of sound advice and assistance and a remarkably calming influence at those times when we despaired ever finishing our task. While recognizing their aid, we must, of course, take responsibility for any flaws in the final product.

Serving as co-editors for this issue was an often difficult but also rewarding experience for us. It was instructive to discover the stresses in our own lives caused by serving as editors of each other's work, as opposed to the more usual and less formal function of critical colleagues. The existence of an official (although reciprocal) status differential, however transitory, is not something that either of us accepted easily. Despite our trials and tribulations we have, in the end, enjoyed putting this issue together. We feel pleased with the papers in the issue and hope that you will find it both interesting and informative.

Rebecca Bryson
Jeff B. Bryson
California State University, San Diego

I Will Follow Him: Myth, Reality, or Forced Choice— Job-Seeking Experiences of Dual-Career Couples

Barbara Strudler Wallston

George Peabody College

Martha A. Foster

North Metro Children's Center, Atlanta

Michael Berger

Georgia State University

Recent PhDs in psychology and biological sciences with spouses who were also professionals were surveyed; the focus was on their joint job-seeking. Couples frequently described egalitarian decision rules. But traditional patterns were also evident, particularly among the biological-science sample. Egalitarianism decreased in the actual job decisions made, but here the traditional alternative was frequently cited as a forced choice. Responses to simulations showed egalitarian decisions to be common under low constraint conditions. Constraints such as the need for a job and time pressure produced more nonegalitarian decisions. However, under these hypothetical conditions, the constraints were as likely to produce nontraditional as traditional following. It is suggested that the high traditionality of actual job decisions is, at least in part, a result of institutional constraints.

Married women have increasingly entered the work force since World War II, and increasing numbers of women are entering profes-

---

This study was supported in part by Biomedical Sciences Support Grant FR-RR07087 from the General Research Support Branch, Division of Research Resources, Bureau of Health Professions, Education and Manpower Training, National Institutes of Health. We would like to thank Marie Epperson, Sue Falsey, Betty Kaiser, and Jane St. John for their invaluable assistance in data collection, coding analysis, and typing. Thanks also to Bob DeVellis, Brenda DeVellis, Diane Kravetz, Kenneth Wallston, and Larry Wrightsman for comments on a draft of this manuscript. Requests for reprints should be sent to Barbara Strudler Wallston, Box 512, George Peabody College, Nashville, Tennessee 37203.

sional fields (Astin, 1967; Bernard, 1971; Hunt, 1968; Oppenheimer, 1973; Suelze, 1970; Wrochno, 1966). Since professional women are very likely to marry males who are also professionals (Astin, 1969; Feldman, 1973), dual-career couples are likely to become more prevalent in western industrial societies (Rapoport & Rapoport, 1971). Recent research has begun to explore a number of issues relevant to such couples including career patterns (Holmstrom, 1971; Rapoport & Rapoport, 1971), family roles (Poloma & Garland, 1971; Rapoport & Rapoport, 1971), professional development (Bryson, Bryson, Licht, & Licht, 1976; Martin, Berry, & Jacobsen, 1975), and marital happiness (Bailyn, 1971). None of these studies, however, has concentrated on job-seeking.

Job-seeking by the head of the household has been shown to be an extremely significant and stressful event for the individual (Fogarty, Rapoport, & Rapoport, 1971; Gross, 1970; Taylor & Chave, 1964; Wilensky, 1966). For couples both involved in this pursuit, it should be even more stressful. Interest in these issues and in new solutions to them is illustrated in treatments of commuting couples in the popular press (e.g., *Time*, July 9, 1973; *New York Times*, November 13, 1972) and in more specialized publications (Lehmann, 1975; Struik, 1974; Westoff, 1973). The fact that arrangements such as commuting and job-sharing (Malan, 1975) are still considered newsworthy suggests that they are infrequent and not modal decisions among dual-career couples. How, then, do such couples search for jobs; how do they make decisions when they receive job offers?

The traditional expectation is that the man's career is more important and, thus, his job takes precedence. Research by Poloma and Garland (1971) showed this to be the case even among the female lawyers, doctors, and academics they studied in 1968 as did Standley and Soule (1974), who studied women in medicine, law, and architecture. Berman, Sacks, and Lief (1975) cited a case that illustrates such decision-making by two doctors choosing internships.

However, some data suggest this is not wholly the case. Holmstrom (1971) showed that professional careers of spouses are mutually interdependent. While in each case the wife's decision about where to live had been significantly influenced by her husband's career, in most cases the husband's decision about where to live had at least once also been significantly influenced by the wife's career. Duncan (1975), in a study of migration data, similarly found that the wife's prestige, income, and the compatibility of her occupation with migration mediated the relationship between family migration and the migration demands of the husband's occupation. Migration demands of the wife's occupation were generally not related to family migration. Similarly, Bryson and Bryson (1975) found a majority of wives willing to accept a job in another town only if their husbands also received satisfactory offers, while only a quarter of the wives would expect the same consideration from their husbands. The choice of long-distance commuting by some couples also shows the relevance of the wife's occupation. Ngai's (1974) interviews with two professional commuting families suggested "that the commuting lifestyle is indeed a feasible way of solving the career coordination problem of two-career families" (p. 2).

This study attempted to explore further job-seeking among dual-career couples. In addition to self-report information gathered on couples' decision rules and actual job selection, we asked people to respond to several simulated job-seeking situations. Thus, we hoped to explore systematically the effects of sex and outside constraints on job-seeking under controlled circumstances that are not possible when studying actual job-seeking behavior.

METHOD

Sample

Recent PhDs in psychology and biological sciences (specifically biochemistry, microbiology, and physiology) were contacted for participation. Names of PhDs between 1972 and 1974 were gathered from letters to 800 department chairpersons. Chairpersons from 57% of the departments responded, and questionnaires were sent to the 1,599 PhDs and their spouses (approximately equally distributed between psychology and biological science) whose names chairpersons supplied. Responses were obtained from 427 couples or 28% (excluding those 94 who could not be located from the base figure). The psychology return rate was slightly higher (33%) than the rate for biological science (18%).

A relatively strict definition of a professional was used to define subjects: having obtained the recognized terminal degree in the person's field. Thus, the final sample consisted of 107 professional couples (214 professionals) in which at least one spouse had a PhD in psychology and 53 professional couples (106 professionals) in which at least one spouse had a PhD in biological science. These represent 13% and 6%, respectively, of psychology and biological science PhDs sent questionnaires. To be eligible for the final sample, the couple must have searched for jobs within the last five years. Most questions were asked regarding the first time the couples searched for a job after both were professionals.

Psychology couples ranged in age from 22 to 60 with a mean of 31.8 (standard deviation = 6.68). References to psychology couples (sample) and biological-sciences couples (sample) include males and females in each of these fields and their spouses who might be in any field. For biological-science couples, the mean age was 31.5 (standard deviation = 5.39) with a range from 26 to 52.

Psychology couples were married a mean of 7.4 years (standard deviation = 6.36), and biological-science couples were married a mean of 6.5 years (standard deviation = 5.39).

Procedure

Two questionnaires were mailed to each couple; spouses were requested to complete them independently. Because questionnaires could be returned anonymously, no follow-up contacts were made to obtain additional responses.

In addition to self-report questions on personal experiences, professionals were given two hypothetical situations to which to respond. For each situation, half the couples received questionnaires in which person A was a female and person B was a male. The other half received questionnaires in which the sexes of A and B were reversed. The simulations are presented in Table 1.

Simulation one presented hypothetical conditions expected to be conducive to egalitarian job seeking. Simulation two introduced the outside constraints of job availability (2A) and time pressure (2B).

Table 1

Simulations

In each of the following hypothetical situations, circle the action you would be most likely to take. All of these assume that both spouses are professionals and are seeking employment. Put yourself in the position of the character whose sex matches yours. Feel free to comment on any of the situations, but please make a single response as well, even if you are unhappy with the choices.

1. Bob (Sue) has received an outstanding job offer. His wife, Sue (Her husband, Bob), has been unable to locate a position in the same geographic area. Both Bob and Sue have received moderately attractive offers in another location which is quite distant from the first. It is relatively late in the year and chances of obtaining alternate positions seem dim.

a. Bob and Sue accept the two offers.

b. Bob (Sue) accepts the more attractive offer and Sue (Bob) comes along, hoping to find something.

c. Bob (Sue) accepts the attractive offer and Sue (Bob) accepts her (his) offer. They will live separately for the time being.

d. They decline all offers and continue looking.

BARBARA STRUDLER WALLSTON, MARTHA A. FOSTER, MICHAEL BERGER

Table 1 (Continued)

2. Mary (Frank) has received a very good job offer, and must make a
decision. Frank (Mary) has not yet received a firm offer, but there
appear to be good possibilities for the future. He (She) can't
arrange interviews before Mary's (Frank's) deadline. Mary (Frank)
may be able to locate another position in the geographic location
in which Frank (Mary) has possibilities.

A. Assume that it's early in the job hunting season, i.e., you've
only been job hunting for a month, and it's six months until you
expect to begin work.

a. Mary (Frank) accepts the job and Frank (Mary) goes to look
for a position in that area.

b. Mary (Frank) declines the job, and they both continue looking.

c. Mary (Frank) accepts the job, and Frank (Mary) pursues his
(her) possibilities, with the chance that they'll live
separately for the time being.

B. Assume that it's late in the year, i.e., two months before you
need to begin work and you've been job hunting for a number of
months. Which of the above alternatives would you now choose?
a   b   c

Note. Form 1 is presented above with Form 2 changes shown in parentheses.

RESULTS AND DISCUSSION

Simulations

Simulation one. In simulation one, form one, a male had an out-standing job offer where his wife was unable to locate a position, while both had moderately attractive offers elsewhere. In form two, it was the female with the outstanding offer. Three egalitarian options were presented, taking the two offers (a), taking offers in separate locations (c), and declining all offers (d). Option (b) was nonegalitarian, with the wife following the husband as is traditionally expected in form one and husband following wife in form two.

Chi square tests contrasting egalitarian and nonegalitarian choices by form were not significant for either psychology ($x^2 = .46$) or biological science ($x^2 = 2.03$). Data are presented in Table 2. For all forms, a high percentage of choices were egalitarian (ranging from 71% to 83%).

Simulation two. Simulation two presented the wife with a very good offer before her husband had anything definite (form one). Participants were asked how they would respond to this situation if it were to occur early in job-hunting (termed Simulation 2a) and then late in job-hunting (Simulation 2b). In form two, the husband had the good offer. Again, for each form, only one nonegalitarian choice was

JOB-SEEKING EXPERIENCES OF DUAL-CAREER COUPLES

Table 2

Simulation 1--Good Joint Alternative

Psychology Sample		
Non-Egalitarian Response Implies:	Non-Egalitarian	Egalitarian
Husband follows (Form 2)	20 (17%)	95 (83%)
Wife follows (Form 1)	23 (26%)	67 (74%)
Biological Science Sample		
Husband follows (Form 2)	12 (23%)	40 (77%)
Wife follows (Form 1)	12 (29%)	29 (71%)

presented—the husband following on form one [option (a)], the wife following on form two. Two egalitarian choices were presented on each form—to continue looking (b) or possibly to live separately to maximize good job possibilities for both (c).

Data contrasting egalitarian and nonegalitarian choices early in the year are presented in Table 3. For the psychology sample, almost half of the choices were egalitarian, and this did not differ by whether the husband or wife would follow in the nonegalitarian choice (x^2 = .07). In the biological-sciences sample, however, there was a significant chi square (x^2 = 8.33, p < .005) showing differential egalitarian choice by form. That is, biological-science respondents made more nonegalitarian choices where this was the traditional choice (wife follows; form two) and fewer nonegalitarian choices where the husband would be following the wife. Again, however, overall there were nearly 50% egalitarian choices.

Table 3

Simulation 2A--Only One Offer Early in Job-Hunting

Psychology Sample		
Non-Egalitarian Response Implies:	Non-Egalitarian	Egalitarian
Husband follows (Form 1)	41 (46%)	49 (54%)
Wife follows (Form 2)	54 (47%)	60 (53%)
Biological Science Sample		
Husband follows (Form 1)	14 (34%)	27 (66%)
Wife follows (Form 2)	34 (64%)	19 (36%)

BARBARA STRUDLER WALLSTON, MARTHA A. FOSTER, MICHAEL BERGER

Table 4

Simulation 2B--Only One Offer Late in Job-Hunting

Psychology Sample

Non-Egalitarian Response Implies:	Non-Egalitarian	Egalitarian
Wife follows (Form 2)	89 (78%)	25 (22%)
Husband follows (Form 1)	65 (75%)	22 (25%)

Biological Science Sample

Wife follows (Form 2)	25 (87%)	7 (13%)
Husband follows (Form 1)	30 (75%)	10 (25%)

Table 4 presents data on the same simulation late in job-hunting. The nonegalitarian choices rose to a range of 75% to 87% where there was only one job offer. Here it was no longer relevant whether the husband or wife must follow for the psychology ($x^2 = 0.31$) or biological-science samples ($x^2 = 1.99$). Thus, we have the forced choice referred to in the title. When the situation in form two occurs it appears, from an outside perspective, like the traditional wife-following-husband situation, but, as presented here, it may be the economic press to find at least one job that necessitates the decision.

Summary of simulation data. The results from the simulations are summarized in Table 5. Overall, there were a great many egalitarian

Table 5

Simulations Contrasted (Tables 2, 3, and 4 Combined)

Data Collapsed Over Forms 1 & 2

	Good Job Alternative Simulation 1	Only One Job Early Simulation 2A	Only One Job Late Simulation 2B	Total
Psychology Sample				
Egalitarian	162 (79%)	109 (53%)	47 (24%)	318 (52%)
Non-Egalitarian	43 (21%)	95 (47%)	154 (76%)	292 (48%)
Biological Science Sample				
Egalitarian	69 (74%)	46 (49%)	17 (19%)	135 (48%)
Non-Egalitarian	24 (26%)	48 (51%)	75 (81%)	147 (52%)

choices (approximately half of all choices), but the proportion of such choices varied by simulation for both psychology and biological science. That is, egalitarian choices were most common when they produced two jobs, as in Simulation one, and least common when it was only the nonegalitarian choice that resulted in a job, as in Simulation 2b. The proportion of egalitarian choices was the same for both psychology and biological-science samples for each simulation.

Egalitarian choices were particularly likely when good alternatives for both spouses existed, as in Simulation one. However, economic necessity reduced egalitarian choices as in Simulation two, late in job hunting, where only the nonegalitarian choice included a definite job offer. Thus, for these hypothetical situations, "I will follow him" was generally a myth for both wife and (if we change it to "I will follow her") husband.

"I will follow him" was a greater reality than was "I will follow her" only for biological-science couples facing simulation 2a. The responses to Simulation 2b for both samples showed that "I will follow him" or "I will follow her" may be a forced choice.

Now we will report on the actual decisions couples made and contrast them with the simulation data.

Actual Decision-Making

Final decision. Couples were asked to characterize their final decision using one of seven categories: (1) the best joint situation, (2) only I had an offer so spouse followed, (3) only spouse had an offer, so I followed, (4) I accepted a good job offer and my spouse followed, (5) spouse accepted a good job offer and I followed, (6) I was already working so spouse followed, or (7) spouse was already working so I followed. These were divided into egalitarian (choice 1), I lead (choices 2, 4, and 6), and I follow (choices 3, 5, and 7), and responses from males and females were contrasted. These data for psychology and biological-science samples are presented in Table 6. The percent of egalitarian final decisions ranged from 21% to 29%, similar to response to Simulation 2b. For both samples, as is traditionally expected, men were more likely to take jobs and lead and women were more likely to follow ($x^2 = 40.19$, P $<$ .001, psychology; $x^2 = 38.23$, $p <$ .001, biological science).

Thus, for final decisions, "I will follow him" appeared to be a reality for a high proportion of female respondents. However, if these

BARBARA STRUDLER WALLSTON, MARTHA A. FOSTER, MICHAEL BERGER

Table 6

Final Job Decision

Who Leads?

	Egalitarian (1)	I Lead (2, 4, 6)	I Follow (3, 5, 7)
Psychology Females	24 (25%)	13 (13%)	60 (62%)
Psychology Males	24 (29%)	43 (52%)	16 (19%)
Biol. Science Females	10 (21%)	5 (11%)	32 (68%)
Biol. Science Males	9 (21%)	29 (67%)	5 (12%)

Note. Since both husband and wife are responding, I lead and I follow should be mirror images for males and females, except for non-respondents. Numbers in parentheses in heading refer to response choices described in the text.

data are further broken down (see Table 7), it can be seen that in a large percentage of the cases (the percent varies with males slightly but not significantly more likely to say this; $x^2 = 2.44$, psychology; $x^2 = 3.10$, biological science) the "I will follow or lead" was a forced choice. That is, only one job was available when the final decision was made. Thus, nonegalitarian choices were more freely made by only about one-third of our sample (with the estimates ranging from 23% to 43%).

Decision rules. Data were also gathered on decision rules couples set up while searching for positions. Respondents were asked to

Table 7

Final Job Decision

Further Categorization

	Egalitarian (1)	Only One Job (2, 3)	Other Non-Egalitarian (4, 5, 6, 7)
Psychology Females	24 (25%)	34 (35%)	39 (40%)
Psychology Males	24 (29%)	34 (41%)	25 (30%)
Biol. Science Females	10 (21%)	17 (36%)	20 (43%)
Biol. Science Males	9 (21%)	24 (56%)	10 (23%)

Note. Numbers in parentheses in heading refer to response choices described in the text.

characterize their decision rules as (1) I look first, then spouse; (2) spouse looks first, then I look; (3) both look independently; (4) both look within a particular area; (5) work out the best joint option; (6) apply as a couple; (7) locate where I had best offer; or (8) locate where spouse had the best offer. Broadly defined, options (3), (4), (5), and (6) can be classified as egalitarian, while (1) and (7) are "I lead" and (2) and (8) are "I follow." Data for males and females are presented in Table 8.

Significant chi squares were obtained for both the biological-science ($x^2 = 28.53, p < .001$) and psychology samples ($x^2 = 13.36, p < .005$). As with the final decision, women were more likely to say "I will follow him." However, a higher percentage of the rules were egalitarian (42% for biological science and 61% for psychology) compared to the final job decision, where job availability constraints restricted choices.

Collapsing over the nonegalitarian rules and comparing the psychology and biological-science samples shows that the psychology couples were significantly more likely ($x^2 = 6.27, df = 1, p < .05$)[2] to choose egalitarian decision rules than were the biological-science couples. (Only the female data were used for this comparison, so as to avoid an artificial inflation of the sample size.) However, the proportion of egalitarian final job decisions by psychology couples was only slightly and not significantly higher (27%) than for science couples (21%). Choosing an egalitarian strategy is only a first step in job-seeking. Making such a strategy work appears to be much more difficult. Institutional constraints, which we will discuss below, ap-

Table 8

Decision Rules

Who Leads

	Egalitarian (3, 4, 5, 6)	I Lead (1, 7)	I Follow (2, 8)
Psychology Females	59 (61%)	10 (10%)	28 (29%)
Psychology Males	60 (61%)	26 (26%)	13 (13%)
Biol. Science Females	20 (39%)	5 (10%)	26 (51%)
Biol. Science Males	22 (46%)	22 (46%)	4 (8%)

Note. Numbers in parentheses in the heading refer to response choices described in the text.

BARBARA STRUDLER WALLSTON, MARTHA A. FOSTER, MICHAEL BERGER

pear to be a major impediment to egalitarian job-seeking by dual-career couples. For recent PhD professional couples, while "I will follow him" is clearly not a myth, it appears to be more of a forced than a desired choice.

Employers should, thus, remember that egalitarian responses were sufficiently frequent so that the casual assumption that a wife will follow her husband is just not warranted.

Institutional Constraints

Job Market. Several questions requested information on how respondents perceived the job market. Respondents were asked to rate the difficulty of finding employment in their fields, from extremely difficult (coded 1) to somewhat difficult (coded 2) to not at all difficult (coded 3). Responses did not differ by sex of subject or by field. Approximately 30% of the respondents answered extremely difficult, and only 10% answered not at all difficult.

Couple constraints. The tight job market could be problematic for any professional seeking a job. We also tried to investigate specific problems for the professional couple.

Open-ended responses characterizing employers' reactions to joint job-seeking were coded as negative, neutral, or positive. Women in the psychology sample were particularly likely to report negative responses ($x^2 = 4.89, df = 1, p < .05$) compared to men in the psychology sample, while biological science reactions did not differ by sex. Overall, only 29% of psychology and 36% of biological–science respondents reported favorable employer reactions.

Responses to "If I weren't married, I would have been able to obtain a better professional position" (ranging from strongly agree, coded 1, to strongly disagree, coded 5) also reflected perceptions of couple constraints. Overall, responses to this question reflected neutral to slight disagreement (biological science = 3.94; psychology = 3.42). However, there were major differences between male and female responses.

A two-way analysis of variance showed a strong main effect for sex ($F = 41.75, df = 1, 301, p < .001$) and no other significant effects. Women were more likely to agree with the statement in both psychology (2.99 vs. 3.88) and biological science (2.96 vs. 4.04) than were men.

Thus, there is some evidence that institutional constraints are seen as specifically hampering professional couples.

JOB-SEEKING EXPERIENCES OF DUAL-CAREER COUPLES

Implications

What are the implications of all this? The most critical relates to employers. They must be educated as to the needs of professional couples and to the fact that "I will follow him" is at least somewhat of a myth or frequently a forced choice. We support Struik's (1974) statement, "When a married female applicant is being considered, it is she and/or her husband who 'own' the problem of the husband's job" (p. 11). Employers' current insistence on considering the husband's situation before making a job offer to his wife is one of the constraints leading to nonegalitarian forced choices. Policy changes and programs to educate employers are needed so that the task of raising their consciousnesses does not fall entirely on the shoulders of dual-career couples seeking employment. Furthermore, given the frequency with which couples cited institutional constraints as hampering their attempts to follow an egalitarian job-seeking strategy, we think it important for dual-career couples to acknowledge the reality of these constraints and not to blame themselves should they fail to find two good or two acceptable positions. Couples who blame themselves or one another for their failure to find two acceptable jobs are, in important ways, blaming the victims of present institutional arrangements.

Lastly, contrary to much previous literature and to popular myth, we found many couples attempting egalitarian or nontraditional (husband follows wife) job-seeking patterns. It may well be time, therefore, for researchers investigating the career development of women to give up their earlier assumptions. It may even be time for researchers investigating the career development of men (as well as the employers of men) to abandon the assumption that professional men will sacrifice the needs of other members of their family to the demands of their career.

REFERENCES

Astin, H. Factors associated with the participation of women doctorates in the labor force. *Personnel and Guidance Journal*, 1967, *46*, 240–246.

Astin, H. *The women doctorate in America*. New York: Russell Sage, 1969.

Bailyn, L. Career and family orientation of husbands and wives in relation to marital happiness. In A. Theodore (Ed.), *The professional women*. Cambridge, Mass.: Schenkman, 1971.

Berman, E., Sacks, S., & Lief, H. The two-professional marriage: A new conflict syndrome. *Journal of Sex and Marital Therapy*, 1975, *1*, 242–253.

Bernard, J. *Women and the public interest*. Chicago: Aldine, 1971.

Bryson, R. B., & Bryson, J. B. *Relative career values of husbands and wives*. Paper presented at the American Psychological Association, Chicago, 1975.

Bryson, R. B., Bryson, J. B., Licht, M. H., & Licht, B. G. The professional pair: Husband and wife psychologists. *American Psychologist,* 1976, *31,* 10–16.

Duncan, R. P. Dual occupational participation and migration. (Doctoral Dissertation. Purdue University.) *Dissertation Abstracts International,* 1975, *36,* 1115A.

Feldman, S. Impediment or stimulant? Marital status and graduate education. *American Journal of Sociology,* 1973, vol. 78, 982–994.

Fogarty, M., Rapoport, R., & Rapoport, R. *Sex, career, and family.* London: George Allen & Unwin, 1971.

Gross, E. Work and stress. In N. Scotch & S. Levine (Eds.), *Social stress.* Chicago: Aldine, 1970.

Holmstrom, L. Career patterns of married couples. In A. Theodore (Ed.), *The professional woman.* Cambridge, Mass.: Schenkman, 1971.

Hunt, A. Survey of women's employment. *Government Social Survey* (London), 1968, *55,* p. 379.

Lehmann, P. Married, moving up, and moving. *Womanpower* (a special issue of *Manpower Magazine*), 1975, *7* (11), 19–24.

Malan, M. Job-sharing couple finds its a corporate ideal. *Nashville Tennessean,* November 27, 1975.

Martin, T., Berry, K., & Jacobsen, R. The impact of dual-career marriages on female professional careers: An empirical test of a Parsonian hypothesis. *Journal of Marriage and the Family,* 1975, *37,* 734–742.

Ngai, S. Y. A. Long-distance commuting as a solution to geographical limitation to career choices of two-career families. Unpublished master's thesis, Cornell University, School of Management, 1974.

Oppenheimer, V. K. Demographic influence on female employment and the status of women. *American Journal of Sociology,* vol. 78 Jan., 1973.

Poloma, M. M., & Garland, T. N. The myth of the egalitarian family: Familial roles and the professionally employed wife. In A. Theodore (Ed.), *The professional woman.* Cambridge, Mass.: Schenkman, 1971.

Rapoport, R., & Rapoport, R. *Dual-career families.* Baltimore: Penguin Books, 1971.

Standley, K., & Soule, B. Women in professions: Historic antecedents and current lifestyles. In R. E. Hardy & J. G. Cull (Eds.), *Career guidance for young women.* Springfield, Ill.: Charles C. Thomas, 1974.

Struik, R. R. The two-city problem. *Association for Women in Mathematics Newsletter,* 1974, *4*(6), 8–11.

Suelzle, M. Women in labor. *Transaction,* 1970, *8,* 50–59.

Taylor, L., & Chave, S. *Mental health and environment.* London: Longsman, Green, & Co., 1964.

Westoff, A. L. The two-career couple. *Princeton Alumni Weekly,* November 27, 1973, 18–19.

Wilensky, H. Work as a social problem. In H. Becker (Ed.), *Social problems: A modern approach.* New York: John Wiley, 1966.

Wrochno, K. Women in directing positions about themselves. *Kobieta Wspolczesna,* 1966. Cited in Rapoport & Rapoport, 1971.

Anti-Nepotism's Ghost: Attitudes of Administrators Toward Hiring Professional Couples

Suzanne Pingree, Matilda Butler, William Paisley, and Robert Hawkins

Stanford University

Laws and policies are often the formalization of attitudes. The attitudes that originally led to the policy *continue* even when the policy no longer exists. We felt the anti-nepotism policies, declared discriminatory by HEW's Office of Civil Rights, were still in effect in the attitudes of college and university faculty. To test this, we surveyed the chairpersons of departments of psychology and sociology concerning their attitudes toward hiring a professional couple in their department. Responses to the question "Overall, how likely is it you would support the hiring of a professional couple?" indicated opposition by 37% of the chairpersons, neutrality by 25%, and support by 38%. When asked to list comments under four headings— advantages to department, disadvantages to department, professional advantages to couple, and professional disadvantages to couple—we found that supporters were more likely than opposers to mention advantages to the department and to the couple and that opposers were more likely than supporters to mention disadvantages to the department and to the couple. The types of comments made by the chairpersons may be useful to academic couples wishing to work together.

"When James J. Gibson, a psychologist, moved from Smith College to Cornell University in 1948, his wife, Eleanor, also a psychologist, applied for a teaching job in her husband's department. Sixteen years later, she was hired....

"When Janet Taylor Spence went to the University of Texas in 1964, she had to forego teaching in the psychology department because her husband was already employed there. Instead she moved into the educational

All authors were at Stanford University at the time the research was conducted. Suzanne Pingree is now at the University of Wisconsin, Women's Studies Program; Matilda Butler is Director of the Women's Educational Equity Communications Network, Far West Laboratory for Educational Research and Development, 1855 Folsom St., San Francisco, California 94103; William Paisley is at Stanford University, Communication Department; Robert Hawkins is at the University of Wisconsin, School of Journalism and Mass Communication. Each of the authors is married to one of the coauthors. Requests for reprints should be sent to Matilda Butler.

Psychology of Women Quarterly, Vol. 3(1) Fall 1978
0361-6843/78/1500-0022$00.95 © 1978 Human Sciences Press

SUZANNE PINGREE, MATILDA BUTLER, WILLIAM PAISLEY, ROBERT HAWKINS

psychology department . . . In 1967 her husband died and she moved into the psychology department. A year later, she was named department chairman."

(San Francisco Chronicle, July 7, 1975, p. 16)

These are two "success stories" of professional couples. In time, the women were hired. But for decades, anti-nepotism policies prevented many qualified wives from seeking teaching positions and caused still others to be denied teaching positions.

It took until June of 1971 for the Board of Directors of the Association of American Colleges to endorse a statement concerning "anti-nepotism regulations" that concluded, "Such policies and practices subject faculty members to an automatic decision on a basis wholly unrelated to academic qualifications and limit them unfairly in their opportunity to practice their profession." More to the point, these rules were called "discriminatory" by HEW's Office of Civil Rights in 1972 because of their effect on "faculty wives." While these statements may have helped clear the air of such discriminatory policies, whether or not the *attitudes* toward hiring married couples in academia have been affected is another question. A university or college with an administrator who is personally opposed to the idea of hiring couples probably has an anti-nepotism policy whether or not it exists in written form.

METHOD

The Questionnaire. Anti-nepotism policies were an institutional version of a prevailing discriminatory attitude toward women. When the formal statement is removed, department chairpersons may go back to relying on their attitudes when making hiring decisions. To better understand attitudes toward hiring couples in the same department, we sent a questionnaire to the chairperson of either the psychology or sociology department of all colleges and universities in the United States.

The questionnaire asked the chairperson to imagine that she or he had two assistant-professor openings for which a wife-husband team had applied. The couple was described as having good recommendations and qualifications and one publication each. Respondents were asked to list their comments in an open-ended format under four headings: advantages to the department, disadvantages to the department, professional advantages to the couple, and professional disadvantages to the couple. An attitude scale ranging from "actively oppose" to "actively support" was also included for responses to the question, "Overall, how likely is it you would support the hiring of a professional couple?"

The Sample. To ensure a reasonable *number* of responses, question-naires were sent to the 2,027 colleges and universities listed in *The College Blue Book* (1969). Half (every other one) were addressed to psychology de-partments and half were addressed to sociology departments. Questionnaires going to the 34 "major" departments (as determined by four judges) were separately coded.

RESULTS

Response Rate. We received completed questionnaires from 329 (16 %) of the department chairpersons. Using the postmark on each returned envelope as an indicator of geographic location, we found we had responses from 46 states and Puerto Rico. Only the "major" university departments were sent a follow-up mailing. This was done in an effort to obtain a useful number of responses in this already small group. As expected, the "major" departments had a higher response rate (62%) than the overall sample.

Response Categories. Categories were developed separately for each of the four open-ended questions on the basis of the respon-dents' comments. Each separate idea was coded, and the question-naires were check-coded three times to ensure uniform use of the categories. Intercoder reliability for a sample was 85%.

The four most frequently mentioned categories for advantages to the department were: (1) the couple's greater unity between personal and professional lives enhancing the department (23%), (2) no advan-tage (19%), (3) the department's greater ability to coordinate faculty professional and research activities (14%), and (4) the department's greater stability of personnel (12%).

Combining all major categories into two main clusters, we find that 36% of the chairpersons mentioned "positive effects from the couple's relationship" and 40% mentioned "administrative and eco-nomic convenience to the department."

The four most frequently mentioned categories for disadvantages to the department were: (1) the department's faculty evaluations being difficult (31%), (2) the couple's marital and emotional problems upsetting the department (22%), (3) the couple's disproportionate or adverse influence on departmental politics (22%), and (4) the couple's dissatisfaction resulting in two vacancies at the same time (18%).

Seven of the frequently mentioned categories can be regrouped into two clusters of problems cited by department chairpersons. We found that "the couple as source of discontent" was mentioned by 45% of the respondents and "administrative problems" were mentioned by 42%.

The major advantages to the couple were: (1) the couple's greater personal life-professional life unity (27%), (2) the couple's better coordination of professional and research activities (27%), (3) the couple's ability to save expenses, resources, and time (16%), and (4) no advantage (10%).

The seven substantive codes for this category were grouped into two major clusters. We found that 45% of the chairpersons mentioned "professional development" and 36% mentioned "economics and conveniences to the couple."

The four most frequently perceived disadvantages to the couple were: (1) the department's effect on the couple's decisions and behavior (17%), (2) the couple's personal competition and jealousy (15%), (3) the couple's inability to maintain separate identities, and (4) the couple's social problems with others, e.g., resentment (10%).

Summary groupings for eight of the codes indicated that 36% of the chairpersons mentioned "professional problems for the couple" and 26% mentioned "marital problems for the couple."

In some ways, those not responding under a particular heading spoke just as loudly as those who did. We found the number of respondents not commenting varied systematically across the four headings, with disadvantages to the department having the smallest number of no responses and professional advantages to the couple and professional disadvantages to the couple having more than would be expected ($x^2 = 18.08$, $df = 3$, $p < .01$). In addition, respondents explicitly stating "no advantage" or "no disadvantage" were more numerous for advantages to the department and less numerous for disadvantages to the department and disadvantages to the couple ($x^2 = 35.65$, $df = 3$, $p < .01$).

Attitude Scale.   Responses to the question "Overall, how likely is it you would support the hiring of a professional couple?" were evenly distributed between oppose and support. We found 16% actively oppose, 21% somewhat oppose, 19% somewhat support, and 19% actively support the hiring of a professional couple. When we group the "somewhat" and "actively" categories, we note that 37% oppose, 25% are neutral, and 38% support the hiring of a couple.

Table 1 shows all coded comments concerning the department or couple by responses of attitude toward hiring a professional

ANTI-NEOPOTISM'S GHOST

Table 1

All Coded Responses[a] Concerning Department

or Couple, by Attitude Toward Hiring

Professional Couple

	Attitude		
	Support	Neutral	Oppose
Advantages to Department	27%	19%	15%
Disadvantages to Department	28	36	42
Advantages to Couple	22	24	20
Disadvantages to Couple	22	21	23
NUMBER	628	340	487

[a] These responses include all codable comments except explicit
"no advantage" and "no disadvantage" comments.

couple. The only comments excluded are explicit statements of "no advantage" or "no disadvantage." We found that of the 628 comments made by supporters of hiring couples, 28% concerned disadvantages to the department, 27% concerned advantages to the department, 22% concerned advantages to the couple, and 22% concerned disadvantages to the couple. Of the 487 comments made by opposers of hiring couples, 42% concerned disadvantages to the department, 23% concerned disadvantages to the couple, 20% concerned advantages to the couple, and 15% concerned advantages to the department. As we would expect, opposers made more comments on disadvantages than on advantages. And although supporters were also more likely to mention disadvantages than advantages overall, we note supporters were more likely than opposers to mention advantages to department (27% vs. 15%) and to couple (22% vs. 20%) and that opposers were more likely than supporters to mention disadvantages to department (42% vs. 28%) and to couple (23% vs. 22%).

SUZANNE PINGREE, MATILDA BUTLER, WILLIAM PAISLEY, ROBERT HAWKINS

Table 2

Responses of "No Advantage" and "No Disadvantage"

to Department or Couple, by Attitude Toward

Hiring a Professional Couple

	Attitude		
	Support	Neutral	Oppose
No Advantage to Department	25%	45%	60%
No Disadvantage to Department	32	17	2
No Advantage to Couple	14	21	31
No Disadvantage to Couple	28	17	7
NUMBER	28	42	55

Table 2 shows the same pattern of responses but with more clarity. In this table, we examine those explicit responses of "no advantage" and "no disadvantage" by response of attitude toward hiring a professional couple. Supporters were more likely to mention no disadvantage to department (32%) or to couple (28%), while opposers were more likely to mention no advantage to department (60%) or to couple (31%). There is a 35-point difference between percent of "no advantage to department" comments made by opposers and supporters (60% vs. 25%) and a 17-point difference between percent of "no advantage to couple" comments made by opposers and supporters (31% vs. 14%). We find supporters have a 30-point spread from opposers in percent of "no disadvantage to department" comments (32% vs. 2%) and a 21-point spread in percent of "no disadvantage to couple" comments (28% vs. 7%).

Table 3 shows the responses to disadvantages to the department by amount of prior experience with professional couples (this table presents the only significant results in the set of four). We find, irrespective of prior experience with professional couples in a department, "couple as clique" is mentioned most frequently (49% of comments by those with experience and 35% of comments by those

Table 3

Responses to Disadvantages to the Department,

by Amount of Prior Experience with

Professional Couples

	Experience	No Experience
Couple as Clique	49%	35%
Problems Between Spouses	20	28
Administrative Problems	28	34
No Disadvantage	4	3
NUMBER	167	435

$$x^2 = 11.19, \ 3df, \ p < .05$$

without experience) and "administrative problems" is mentioned next (28% of comments by those with experience and 34% of comments by those with no experience). However, administrators with experience are more likely and administrators without are less likely to mention "couple as clique" than would be expected statistically.

DISCUSSION

Our study indicates that the once formal anti-nepotism rules are kept alive in the attitudes of many chairpersons. We find that although a third of the department chairpersons will support the hiring of a professional couple, the job-hunting wife-husband team is equally likely to be greeted with opposition. There seem to be no real differences in the attitudes expressed by chairpersons from major or minor universities. However, due to faculty-size differences, couples are more likely to find joint positions in the major departments. This supposition is based on our finding that more major than minor departments have had couples on their faculty.

SUZANNE PINGREE, MATILDA BUTLER, WILLIAM PAISLEY, ROBERT HAWKINS

Couples and other interested persons will want to derive their own conclusions from our results, but perhaps some of the potential problems and advantages have been made clearer. Chairpersons from psychology and sociology departments in 46 states made many comments that indicate their belief systems continue to operate as a barrier to hiring couples desiring employment in the same academic department.

The department wanting to avoid discriminatory hiring attitudes and the couple wanting joint employment may find it useful to consider the personal and departmental advantages/disadvantages of the situation. For the couples, we feel a fruitful strategy is to point out and reinforce the positive points concerning the department and the couple that our respondents have mentioned while dealing openly with any serious negative effects. For the department, we urge the chairperson and search committee to consider how their attitudes may be affecting their recruitment of new staff. Serious concerns about the department and the couple should be brought explicitly to the attention of the applicants. We feel most concerns can be dealt with by the parties in a nonprejudicial manner.

What of couples seeking employment in other disciplines? Our findings have been replicated in a study of chairpersons of journalism/communication departments (Pingree & Butler, 1976). With few exceptions, this second group of respondents mentioned the same categories and with the same relative frequency. Although a single replication does not argue for a general application of our findings across all fields, we believe many of the social sciences would have similar concerns.

The number of professional couples seeking employment in the same academic department is statistically small. But as today's academic job market grows smaller, this avenue of research has implications for job-sharing of positions. As more jobs are filled by two persons, rather than one, it will be important to understand the positive and negative beliefs affecting hiring and the positive and negative effects on the two persons and on the department.

REFERENCES

Board of Directors of the Association of American Colleges. *AAUP Bulletin,* Summer, 1971.
Changing times—the nepotism rule. *San Francisco Chronicle,* July 7, 1975, p. 16.
CCM Information Corporation. *College blue book, 1969–1970.* New York: Author, 1969.
Pingree, Suzanne, & Butler, Matilda. "Attitudes toward hiring professional couples in schools and departments of journalism." *Journalism Educator,* accepted for publication, 1976.

Continuous Dual-Career Families: A Case Study

Donald St. John-Parsons

Bank Street College of Education

Intensive studies of the careers, family backgrounds, marital relation-ships, and domestic patterns of 10 continuous dual-career families (i.e., those where the wives interrupted their professional careers only minimally to have children) were made through an in-depth guided-interview ap-proach. It was found that there was little integration of work situations, that the parents experienced severe overload problems, that kinship ties loosened and social life decreased. The wives, usually only children, came from a higher social and economically wealthier class than their husbands; they reverted to traditional sociocultural perceptions of their roles at home but, despite multiple role-cycling dilemmas, found that the intellectual and psychological benefits of their lifestyles far outweighed any disadvantages. Financial gain was not of motivational significance, and the dual-career pattern was not always financially rewarding. The families' child-rearing philosophies were similar, and there was no evidence to suggest that the children experienced any disadvantages caused by their parents' career pat-tern. All families were noticeably healthy and physically active.

The traditional view of occupations and the family presupposes that only one of the conjugal pair will have a career that is highly demanding of time and commitment. Until the addition of children to the dyad, society appears prepared to accept a modification of its view and permits both partners to continue their full-time profes-sional careers without considering the dyad deviant. However, with

---

This study originated from a doctoral dissertation conducted at Teachers College, Colum-bia University. Sincere thanks are due Rhona and Robert N. Rapoport of the Institute of Family and Environmental Research, London, England, the pioneers of research into continuous dual-career families, for their unstinted cooperation as well as generous permission to use their interview guide. Requests for reprints should be sent to Donald St. John-Parsons, Graduate Programs Division, Bank Street College, 610 West 112th Street, New York, New York 10025.

Psychology of Women Quarterly, Vol. 3(1) Fall 1978
0361-6843/78/1500-0030$00.95 © 1978 Human Sciences Press

the addition of children to the unit, one of the parents is usually expected to give up or considerably modify his/her career. In practice, it is almost invariably the woman who makes the modification. Caser and Rokoff (1971) see this as a "logical sequence of women's cultural mandate which prescribes that their primary allegiance be to the family and that men be its providers of both economic means and social status" (p. 535).

The functional significance of restricting the equal opportunity of women to employment has been detailed by Parsons (1954) who, while considering that it is possible for women to follow the same career patterns as men, says:

It is, however, notable that in spite of the very great progress of the emancipation of women from the traditional domestic pattern only a very small fraction have gone very far in this direction. It is also clear that its generalization would only be possible with profound alterations in the structure of the family. (p. 96)

Holstrom (1971) challenges Parsons's views and points out that such "generalization would be possible with profound alterations in the structure of occupations" (p. 25), and she sees no reason to assume that it would be the family system rather than the occupational system that would change. The probable importance of husbands' career and family orientations to marital happiness has been studied by Bailyn (1970), who hypothesized "that an educated, married woman's resolution of the career-family dilemma cannot be adequately evaluated without knowledge of her husband's resolution—of the way he fits his work and his family into his life" (p. 97).

If a dual-career family is defined as one where both heads of the household pursue their professional careers and at the same time maintain a family life together that includes children, then this family pattern is a minority one in our culture. It is deviant in the sense that our culture presupposes that only one spouse will be involved, on a more or less exclusive basis, with the care of home and children, and that that spouse will be female. The latter viewpoint has strong social, institutional, and cultural support, including that of a number of child-care experts.

The Rapoports (1971) discovered three broad work patterns among graduate women:

"conventional" where the woman drops her career when she marries or has children, "interrupted" where the woman stops working when the children are small but intends to resume her career later, and "continuous" where the woman interrupts her career only minimally, or not at all, when she has children. (p. 20)

The present study concentrated on the "continuous" pattern, not only because it is the minority pattern and occurs with little precedent in social history, but because it is a creative pattern in need of investigation that is relatively objective and systematic.

METHOD

Intensive studies were made of the careers, family backgrounds, marital relationships, and patterns of 10 continuous dual-career families.

A guided-interview approach, based on an instrument constructed by Rapoport and Rapoport (1971), was used to gather information. This helped ensure not only that the information gathered from each family would be comparable, but also that comparisons could be made with the British study. While the guide was not in questionnaire form, it followed a detailed and structured format.

Subjects

The 20 participants embraced 14 different professions and included two psychiatrists, an actuary, a minister, five academics drawn from different disciplines, two entrepreneurs, a medical illustrator, a social-science researcher, a television producer, a psychotherapist, a lawyer, a public-school teacher, a sculptor, a lawyer-accountant, and a research geneticist. The mean individual salary was $19,500 and the mean family income $38,500.

The mean age of the males was 41, and of the females, 38. The 10 families had a total of 20 children, 11 female and nine male; the mean number of children per family was two and the mean age seven years, six months.

Procedure

The families were located through a combination of professional and social contacts, and the initial approach to each couple was made by telephone. Usually the spouse with whom contact was made agreed to discuss the project with his/her partner and then to inform the interviewer of their decision. Where preliminary agreement was reached, a meeting was then arranged between the couple and the interviewer at which copies of the interview instrument were made available and discussed.

Subsequent interviews, with one partner at a time, were conducted at the convenience of the families. These generally took place in the couple's home, which also permitted contact with the children. All the interviews were taped and relevant portions were transcribed. The taping usually required two or three sessions and, when items were not clear at the transcription stage, another interview or telephone call was arranged. Frequently the husband, wife, and interviewer met together after a taping session for further discussion.

RESULTS AND DISCUSSION

Integration of Work Situations

While it might seem that the partners in dual-career families would be inclined to integrate their respective work situations to a high degree so that their professional lives would be compatible enough to allow for mutual support and accommodation, the individuals in this study did not support such a hypothesis. In almost every case they seemed to have attempted to find ways that would minimize the need for such integration.

Of the 10 families, seven had practically no integration and, even in one family where two teaching professors were married to each other, there was a marked lack of this factor. Further, in only five families did the partners show any real interest in each other's work, and in four of these it was almost minimal. Only in one family was there genuine enthusiasm about the other's work and friendship with his or her work colleagues. On the other hand, it also has to be recorded that the individuals interviewed for this study did not expect much interest from their partners anyway.

Inevitably, there were times, such as emergencies, when integration was vital; even so, it was not achieved without friction and, almost without exception, it was the woman who made the accommodation.

Division of Household Tasks

In order to generate a picture of the internal family structures, information was obtained by examination of 20 common household tasks.

Although husbands and wives were questioned separately, their replies coincided closely and differences were insignificant. These replies showed that each of the 20 tasks discussed was invariably undertaken by the partner who decided that it needed doing; when this was not so, there was no evidence of coercion of the one per-forming the task by the one who made the decision.

Domestic help. The nine couples who had domestic help gen-erally left the hiring decision to the wife or made a joint decision on the matter, and no dissatisfactions were expressed.

Routine food shopping. This was undertaken by the wives in eight families, by the husband in one, and jointly in one.

Preparation of everyday and special meals. Everyday meals were prepared by the wives in nine and by a housekeeper in one of the families. A few husbands showed interest in special meals but, since none of the families entertained much, led active social lives, or had many children, these occasions were few and far between.

Special household purchases. Such purchases were usually made by both partners but, in several cases, the determination of which one should make the purchase depended on the partner with the greater knowledge about or interest in the item being purchased. There were no cases of friction where this approach was adopted.

Cleaning the house Cleaning was almost entirely undertaken by the domestic help, although the partners in two of the families shared this task. However, one husband positively enjoyed house cleaning, as he found it conducive to thought.

Washing clothes. No husbands washed the clothes by them-selves, although in one family the partners shared this duty. Three wives performed this task themselves, and the rest left it to their domestic help.

Ironing and mending. All families reported that there was little, if any, ironing and mending, and, apart from one wife, none saw it as of any significance; however, while three wives undertook what little there was, no husband attempted these chores.

Household maintenance. In five families this was undertaken by the wife and in five others by the husband, though one wife who had considerable mechanical ability used it only in her work. However, since most families lived in apartments, there was rarely much main-tenance, and families tended to call in superintendents when necessary. In the three families living in their own houses, two husbands undertook the maintenance, while the wife undertook it in the third.

Gardening. Gardening was practically negligible; two wives did this and one husband, but he also brought in hired help.

Care of the car. Of the eight families with cars, six were taken care of by husbands and two by wives; however, any major item was handled by a garage.

Preparation of children for school. As some of the children were old enough to prepare themselves for school, the replies to questions about the performance of this task were not so clear-cut as were most of the others; however, in those families where the parents were still responsible for this task, seven wives or domestic help prepared the children, one couple shared the task, and in another, where the child was an infant, the husband did it but his wife selected the clothes before she left for work.

Transportation to and from school. Transportation was of little importance since most of the children walked to school; however, in two families the partners shared this task, in one the husband undertook it, and in the other the wife transported the children to school.

Care of children in emergencies or illness. Not one husband took sole care of the children in emergencies or illness, although four couples shared this responsibility. Where the families had hired helpers, they were invariably brought in. In the two families where the husbands were physicians, though specialists in psychiatry, the wives took sole care of sick children.

Care of children on school holidays. A similar picture emerged with respect to the care of children during the school holidays among the eight families where this was required. While three wives took sole charge of the children during holidays, not one husband solely undertook this responsibility, though four shared it with their wives. In several cases the domestics supplemented the parents' care. It was not unusual for the wives to take their children to work on school holidays, and this was not seen as a burden or a necessity but as an opportunity to expose them to the picture of their mothers' work and responsibilities. No fathers took their children to work.

Preparation of children for bed.   Six wives prepared children for bed, two couples shared this task, sometimes the domestic helpers were used, and in two families the children were old enough to manage by themselves. One of the fathers with older children regretted the passing of this stage, which he found personally rewarding since he enjoyed reading the bedtime stories.

Disciplining.   None of the families left the disciplining of the children to one partner alone: Eight shared this responsibility, and in two cases the children were too young to be disciplined. Most families worked on the principle of the parent nearest at hand doing the disciplining, and there was no case of one parent delaying discipline until the other arrived home. However, there was evidence that, in several families, the parents disagreed over the amount of discipline the other administered. In one family the husband felt that he should be the disciplinarian but, in practice, and it may have been because the child was so young, he was extraordinarily permissive.

Holiday planning and organization.   Six of the couples planned and organized their holidays together, two left it to the husbands, one left it to the wife, and in one case the question was not applicable.

Service personnel.   A simple pattern did not emerge over the selection of service personnel. On the whole there was joint agreement, but the women selected their own gynecologists and, similarly, the filling of other specialized needs was determined by the interested party.

Finances.   There was no predominant pattern of financial management. Three families did no budgeting, three husbands did it alone, one wife did it herself, and three families shared it. In several families the wives were not as involved as they felt they should have been, but they were not prepared to make an issue of it.

Child care.   Every family shared real concern over child care and most of them had struggled through a variety of expedients and, even so, few were entirely satisfied with their current solutions. Perhaps most extreme was the case of one wife who had interviewed 40 applicants before selecting one to look after her child.
The solutions to the problem of child care fell into four categories: live-in staff used by two families, full-time daily staff used

by six families, part-time staff used by one family, and a full-time infant center used by one family.

The Rapoports' (1971) study showed wide differences among the couples studied in their general philosophy of child rearing, particularly as it relates to the conception held of the child's role in family life. Their findings are not those of this study where, although most families had not formally thought their philosophy through, they had largely similar views on child rearing. They were concerned that their children should have a meaningful family life and, although they could be described as easygoing, there was little, if any, permissiveness. Although so many families had paid domestic help, there was no attempt to inculcate or permit a superior attitude on the part of the children; in fact, those children who were old enough were expected to accept responsibility for themselves and participate in family chores. Probably the one factor that stood out clearest in these family relationships was respect and individual consideration for one another with an extension, where applicable, to the domestic staff.

Personal Motivation

Family backgrounds of wives and husbands. It is clear that, in this study, the families were not uniform in their composition or in the motivations that had produced their lifestyles. However, there were themes that appeared to transcend individual variations.

The wives tended to be only children and, where they had siblings, they were few in number. If the siblings were of the same sex, there was, in every case, severe rivalry.

The majority of wives came from families in which there had been a lack of familial harmony or where there had been tension. This does not imply that they had not been loved or supported; in fact, they usually had had a good relationship with one parent or a relative, but their families had not been relaxed or even comfortable to live with.

The husbands did not come from such emotionally tense homes, but five of them were only children and the others did not come from large families. However, almost without exception, they came from economically poor families and were of a lower social class than their wives.

Ways in which each other's activities were mutually meaningful. Although in most families it was not economically essential that

CONTINUOUS DUAL-CAREER FAMILIES: A CASE STUDY

the wife follow the dual-career pattern, it was of considerable importance in more affective and subjective ways. Most of the partners felt that they were in a creative relationship with each other and that they positively enjoyed their lifestyle despite its inevitable disagreements and conflicts. In several cases the husbands felt it essential that their wives should have an identity outside the family.

While several of the husbands would have preferred their wives to work a little less intensively, they all approved and actively encouraged them to pursue their careers. This approval and encouragement meant a great deal to their wives, particularly those who had guilt feelings about the possible effects of their work on the children.

Resolution of conflicts over which partner's career should take precedence. All of the families suffered such conflicts, particularly in the years immediately following the birth of the first child. Those couples who had been married the longest reported that they had largely resolved the problem, but there was no single, simple resolution. Some families agreed right from the beginning that neither partner's career would be subservient to the other's.

There was no evidence of rivalry or envy on the part of the husbands in those cases where the wives were playing the dominant career role. They were able to accept this without rancor, even where their wives were largely supporting the family financially. It was apparent that the men had strong self-images as well as the ability to identify with their wives in mutual support of their families.

Strains

All families experience strains, and those living in complex metropolitan cities appear to be subject to some peculiar to their environment. However, the urban continuous dual-career families in this study showed that their continued existence committed them to a continuum of strains probably not experienced in other family patterns.

Overload. Every family interviewed experienced work overload problems caused by the fact that neither partner was at home to undertake the conventional domestic duties as well as the care of the children and the arrangement of social activities. These problems varied in intensity and length, sometimes affecting husband and wife alternately as their job demands fluctuated, but sometimes varying as domestic crises occurred.

No one technique for handling the overload problem evolved from the interviews, and most families had tried various approaches. The most common technique was to employ paid domestic staff, but this was rarely as easy as it might appear. These professional families had high standards and expectations, and the staffs they hired rarely met their exacting requirements. Even the use of au pairs was not always successful, since the young women had not been interviewed by the receiving families before arrival in the United States and they only stayed a year or two before returning home. Sometimes the parents found that domestic staff could ease their physical overload but not the emotional strain caused by concern for their children.

Any extra domestic work involved was invariably absorbed by the parents, thus cutting still further into the little leisure or free time they had. This led, in every family, to a narrowed circle of friends and, usually, to a loosening of kinship ties. There was a marked lack of social activities, limited attendance at professional meetings and, with only one exception, little religious activity outside the home. Each family was fiercely independent and determined to be as self-sufficient as possible.

When discussing the problems of overloading, it became apparent that a sine qua non of every family was good health, not only for the parents but also for the children. In addition, they were noticeably energetic and active and, not surprisingly, most reported periods of complete physical exhaustion but not of mental depression. Both parents and children seemed to have developed an inner strength and resilience.

Environmental sanctions. Fogarty, Rapoport, and Rapoport (1971) consider that the women in their study "had to deal with dilemmas arising from the clash between their personal norms (i.e., what they felt was right and proper behavior for themselves) and social norms (i.e., the norms they felt that people around them held)" (p. 352). While these dilemmas were found in the wives studied in this present research, they were by no means as significant as they were for their British counterparts.

It was apparent from this study that, although the couples led socially restricted lives with a limited number of friends, these friends were very close to them. It is most probable that these friends had been selected, perhaps unconsciously, because they were supportive and understanding and because they provided an atmosphere in which the dual-career wives could be comfortable.

Personal identity and self-esteem. While a few of the husbands had experienced dilemmas of identity and self-esteem, particularly in the early years of marriage, they were of little significance when compared with those of most of the wives in this study.

The husbands had maintained traditional sex roles in choosing their culturally masculine professions, whereas the wives, in at least five cases, had, in their careers, crossed conventional sex barriers. On the other hand, although the wives were "advanced" in the sense of having full-time careers as well as children, they reverted, after work, to the sociocultural perception of the wife's role—caring for the home and family.

Understandably, the husbands had few problems of identity and self-esteem, since they maintained culturally acceptable roles both at home and work.

Social-network dilemmas. Although each couple's social-network pattern necessarily differed and was affected by personal circumstances, professional relationships, service relationships, obligations, and a host of other variables, not one family maintained extensive social relationships.

While in most cases their careers were demanding and usually involved a strong sense of commitment, the salient reason for their social dilemmas was their sense of responsibility for and devotion to their children. Several families called in relatives, usually the wife's mother, for help, but none of the families felt comfortable with this arrangement.

Kin relationships deteriorated when the dual-career couples found that they were simply unable to meet the traditional social obligations and expectations of their society. Both husbands and wives reported this loosening of kinship ties, but the husbands appeared to experience the greater loss as their ties with their families of orientation weakened.

The same sort of dilemma arose with other relationships, since, although at first the couples wished to retain them, the sheer overload problem made extensive friendships virtually impossible. Those friends who were retained were few in number, very close, and generally professional families with growing children.

The dual-career families in this study rarely complained about these social-network dilemmas and accepted them as an inevitable characteristic of their chosen lifestyle.

Dilemmas of multiple role-cycling. In a conventional family structure, the family cycle typically supports the husband's work cycle because, even at the time he is establishing himself in his profession, he is relieved of domestic strain. His wife is not engaged in her own professional career and, later, if they do have children, she is available to look after them.

In dual-career families, the domestic and career roles do not fit this pattern of mutual exclusion: Both partners simultaneously pursue careers and manage a home life—a fact that contains the germ of role conflict. In this study it was found that most couples had attempted to establish themselves professionally before having children, thus easing potential conflict to some degree. Those who were successful were, of course, better able to finance the support services their children necessitated. Where children were born before the parents had established themselves professionally, considerable role dilemmas occurred. Nonetheless, in all cases, when the children were born, and most were planned for, the couples rarely even thought about the possibility of the wife's dropping out of a career or of either partner lightening a professional load.

Gains for Husbands and Wives

Self-expression. Many of the dual-career families obviously enjoyed the challenge of their lifestyle; it might have left them exhausted but it also brought them a sense of elation at having successfully overcome a series of dilemmas and crises.

The women particularly felt that they had gained in self-expression and self-esteem, and this theme was dominant in all their interviews. The intellectual and psychological benefits experienced directly by the women and indirectly by their families cannot be underestimated.

While the majority of those studied did not regard financial reward as a major factor, almost all of them did, in fact, have well paying careers.

In addition to an adequate income, at least 12 individuals had occupations that provided a great deal of job security. Without one member of a dual-career family having this security it would have been extremely difficult for them to live their often complicated lives and to provide the care they believed their children needed.

However, the dual-career pattern was not necessarily financially rewarding, since one family spent over half its income on child care, and several others experienced severe financial strains.

Gains for Children

It has been traditional to accept the idea that the children of a working mother are deprived of certain advantages when compared with children of a mother who stays at home. However, this belief is not substantiated by research that indicates that while there are indeed effects, they are not necessarily negative. As Nye and Hoffman (1963) point out, "The effects may be good, bad, or incapable of evaluation; and they may depend on a multitude of other considerations" (p. 210).

Any comments on the characteristics of the children in this study are necessarily subjective, but from the parents' reports and direct observations it appeared that the children were independent, resourceful, and self-confident. In some cases the mothers had a tendency to overcompensate when they came home from work, but they were aware of this behavior and in no sense could any of the children be called "spoiled." Those who were old enough had regular household duties, and they accepted these as their fair contribution to the family pattern. They showed considerable pride in their mothers' careers, and the occasional complaints they had were of a temporary nature.

There was no evidence to suggest that the children would have gained any further benefits had their parents followed a more conventional family structure, and there was definitely nothing to indicate that these children were deprived in any sense of the word.

REFERENCES

Bailyn, L. Career and family orientation of husbands and wives in relation to marital happiness. *Human Relations,* 1970, *23,* 97–113.

Caser, R. L., & Rokoff, G. Women in the occupational world: Social disruption and conflict. *Social Problems,* 1971, *18,* 535–554.

Fogarty, M. P., Rapoport, R., & Rapoport, R. N. *Sex, career and family.* London: George Allen & Unwin, 1971.

Holstrom, L. L. Intertwining career patterns of husbands and wives in certain professions (Doctoral dissertation, Brandeis University, 1971). *Dissertation Abstracts International,* 1970, *31/06A,* 3055A. (University Microfilms No. 70-24637)

Nye, F. I., & Hoffman, L. W. *The employed mother in America.* Chicago: Rand McNally, 1963.

Parsons, T. Age and sex in the social structure of the United States. In *Essays in sociological theory* (Rev. ed.). New York: Free Press, 1954.

Rapoport, R., & Rapoport, R. N. *Dual-career families re-examined.* New York: Colophon Books, 1977.

The Employment Pattern of Professional Couples and Their Distribution of Involvement in the Family

Kathy Weingarten

Harvard University

Thirty-two two-profession couples in three different age groups with children were interviewed together to determine if there was a relationship between their employment pattern and their distribution of family involvement in the home. The couples followed one of two employment patterns: a similar employment history (SEH) in which both people had worked full-time and continuously and a dissimilar employment history (DEH) in which the husband had worked full-time and continuously but the wife had worked part-time. Their involvement in the home was measured by an 80-item interview that covered two modes of interaction in four task areas. Significant differences were found in the ways SEH and DEH couples allocated tasks. Of particular interest was the breakdown of an equitable distribution of tasks in the area of childcare for SEH couples. It was suggested that couples "negotiate" a division of labor that allows women to compensate for the time they spend away from the children and men to choose the family work that is less threatening to their masculine selves.

In 1975, 47.4% (*Monthly Labor Review,* 1975) of all American women with children 18 years of age and younger were in the labor force. As Myrdal and Klein (1956) have stated, the employment of mothers is no longer a secondary role option but must be viewed as a second primary role.[1] What is the impact of this development on the

---

Requests for reprints should be sent to Kathy Weingarten, Department of Psychology, Wellesley College, Wellesley, Massachusetts.
[1]The author is grateful to Dr. Joseph Pleck for bringing Myrdal and Klein's phrase to her attention.

couple? Has participation in the functioning of the family become a second primary role for the husband? Or has the wife simply added work outside the home to the family and householding tasks she already performs? This paper reports on a study done in the Boston metropolitan area in 1973 of the family involvement of one group of two-worker couples in which the husbands are employed full-time as professionals and the wives are professionally employed either full-time or part-time. Although this group constitutes a relatively small proportion of all two-worker couples, it is a group in which one might expect to observe emerging trends (Rapoport & Rapoport, 1969).

Bahr (1974), in a recent review of questionnaire and interview data on marital division of labor, concluded that when a woman is employed, her husband's household labor increases, while hers decreases. Regardless of employment status, though, he found that the primary responsibility for household work still rests with the wife. A study by Holmstrom (1972) of 27 professional couples who differed only in the employment experience of the wives reached similar conclusions. The 20 husbands whose wives had maintained their professional careers "helped" their wives because they saw no other way of accomplishing the family work. The seven husbands whose wives had stopped their careers participated much less in household work.

Other studies of professional couples do not corroborate these findings. Poloma and Garland (1971b) found a range of household participation for the husbands in their sample of 53 currently employed professional couples. Although one couple shared all the family work by equally dividing housework and childcare, in 38% of the couples the husbands did virtually no householding, leaving it entirely to the wife and hired help. Safilios-Rothschild's (1970a) Greek study data are in agreement with Poloma and Garland's (1971b) data, suggesting that when income is high, the wife's employment may not lead to an increase in the husband's household activity, since the couple can afford to hire help.

Time-budget data collected from a range of occupational groups are another source of information that refutes the questionnaire and interview data finding that husbands increase their household activity in response to their wives' employment. In a 1967–68 study of 1,296 husband-wife families in Syracuse, New York, Walker (1970) found that the amount of time husbands contributed to household work and child care did not increase as their wives spent more hours in paid employment. Data from the 1965–66 U.S. portion of the Multi-National Time-Use study reported by Robinson (forthcoming, 1977) substantially support Walker's finding.

Both of these time-budget studies investigated the relative proportion of housework to childcare done by husbands. Contrary to Bahr's (1974, p. 184) conclusion that husbands get "particularly involved" in child care, the time-budget studies revealed the opposite. Child care constituted between one-sixth and one-fourth of the husband's total family work, the majority being devoted to housework.

The study to be reported here undertook to explore the relationship between the employment pattern of professional couples and their distribution of involvement in the home, retaining the comprehensive accounting technique of the time-budget method in combination with the more personal approach of the interview studies. Two aspects of involvement in the home were delineated. The first is the context in which the involvement manifests itself and the second is the nature of the involvement itself.

If a family is to survive, certain tasks must be performed—usually by the couple, who are the family's executive agents. The couple negotiate—whether implicitly or explicitly, once, regularly, or continuously—how they will meet their family's needs. Duvall's (1957) eight basic tasks and Hess and Handel's (1959) five essential processes provided the basis for the four comprehensive task areas that were designed for this study. The four task areas are: (1) meeting each other's psychological and sexual needs; (2) attending to the mechanics of living together; (3) maintaining relations with the community, defined as friends, relatives, neighbors, and community institutions; and (4) raising children.

These four task areas provide the structure within which the couple's involvement, or interaction, with each other can express itself. The study focuses on two modes of interaction of particular relevance to couples: participation and interdependence. As conceptualized in this study, participation measures the contribution of each spouse to the work involved in meeting the family's needs. The couple's division of labor as well as their allocation of resources is covered. Interdependence differs from participation in that it assesses more personal dimensions of the couple's life and deals with the degree to which the couple rely on each other to accomplish tasks, share decision-making, and respond to individual concerns.

METHOD

Subjects

The sample consisted of 32 two-profession couples with children, drawn from a larger set of 54 two-profession couples interviewed. In three instances the husbands did not hold professional degrees, but were in high-level positions in business. Because the employment history of the husbands was not a focus of the study, the educational backgrounds was not controlled as strictly as that of the wives. In 18 of the couples, the husband and the wife had a similar employment history (SEH). That is, both had worked full-time and continuously since receiving their professional degrees. Criteria for this pattern (SEH) were that both members of the couple worked more than 28 hours per week with no more than three consecutive months away from paid work. There were six similarly employed couples in each of three age groups: 28–31, 36–41, and 50–63.

The other 14 couples had a dissimilar employment history (DEH). In this employment pattern, the husbands had worked full-time and continuously since completing their professional training, but the wives had worked either part-time (less than 28 hours per week) and/or discontinuously (taking more than three months off from paid work). Among the DEH couples all the wives were currently employed part-time, and all had children. There were six, five, and three couples respectively in each of the age groups listed above.

Half of the sample was located by a random sampling of the organizational lists of the American Medical Association, the American Bar Association, and the Harvard and MIT alumni offices. The remaining 16 couples were identified through a network-sampling approach. Potential sample couples were identified by means of the woman's name and occupation, because a much larger proportion of professional women are married to professional men than vice-versa.

Measures

A structured interview comprised of 80 questions covering the four task areas and the two modes of interaction was developed. The 20 questions pertaining to the task area of psychological and sexual needs were presented as paper-and-pencil items. All other questions were presented orally.

Each question in the family-involvement matrix (see Table 1) was assigned a value of 0 or 1. The value of "1" was given to the wife if the couple indicated that the wife was more involved in the area covered by the question, to the husband if his involvement was greater, and a point to each if their involvement was equal. The question was given a value of "0" if neither the husband nor wife was involved in that topic area.

The structured interview was taped, and scoring was done from the audiotape of each interview. A standard percentage method (Atkinson, 1958) was used to calculate interscorer reliability, which was 92.6%.

Procedure

With two exceptions, the interview took place in the couple's home during the fall of 1973. The interviewer sat near the tape recorder, approxi-

Table 1: Family Involvement Matrix with Sample Questions

INTERACTION MODES

		Participation	Interdependence
TASK AREAS	Meeting each others psycho- logical and sex- ual needs	Do you give the same amount of encourage- ment to your spouse that s/he gives you?	Does your spouse leave you alone when you want to be left alone?
	Attending to the mechanics of living together	Who spends more time on car repairs?	What personal maintenance tasks does each of you do for the other, for instance hand laundry?
	Maintaining relations with the community	When entertaining friends, who does more of the work?	Does each of you attend social functions that are primarily with friends or work associates of the other?
	Raising children	Who does more car- pooling or trans- porting of children?	Who makes the decisions about whether a child can have a part- icular toy or watch T.V.?

mately equidistant from the husband and wife. The sessions began with the oral presentation of 60 questions followed by the 20 paper-and-pencil items. During the oral interview, the interviewer asked the couple to resolve all disagreements over the accurate answer to a question. The interview took from 35 minutes to 2½ hours, with an average time of 1¼ hours.

RESULTS

A 2x3x2x4x2 (employment by age by people by task by mode) repreated measures analysis of variance was performed on the data: 16 family involvement scores for each of the 32 couples. Significant main and interaction effects were revealed for the between portion of the analysis. The main effects are employment, $F(1,52)=6.64$, $p <.03$; age, $F(2/52)=3.97$, $p <.04$; and people, $F(1,52)=97.19$, $p <.001$. Couples with a similar employment history, couples 28-31, and wives express significantly more family involvement than couples with a dissimilar employment history, couples 36-41 or 50-63, and husbands, respectively.

THE EMPLOYMENT PATTERN OF PROFESSIONAL COUPLES

The employment-by-people interaction, F $(1,52)=27.28$, p $<.001$, shows that whereas SEH husbands do a greater proportion of the family work investigated than DEH husbands, there is no significant difference between SEH and DEH wives in the proportions of family work they do. A Tukey's HSD test (critical value 0.69, p $<.01$) applied to the means reveals that all comparisons of means are significantly different with the exception of the wives' means.

The within portion of the analysis revealed a significant main effect for Task, F $(3,156)=9.76$, p $<.001$, three significant two-way interactions, four significant three-way interactions, and one significant four-way interaction. The interaction of employment by people by task, F $(3,156)=5.08$, p $<.001$, will be reported here as it bears most directly on the topic of this paper; means relevant to this interaction are presented in Table 2. Tukey's HSD test (critical values 1.14, p $<.05$; 1.31, p $<.01$) applied to the means relevant to the question of the relationship between employment pattern and the distribution of family involvement demonstrates the following signficant contrasts: (1) DEH wives' proportion of family work is greater than SEH wives' only in the task area of the mechanics of living together, (2) SEH husbands' proportion of the family work is greater than DEH husbands' in the task areas of the mechanics of living together and child care, (3) DEH wives do a greater proportion of family work than their husbands in all but the task area of meeting each other's psychological and sexual needs, and (4) SEH husbands and wives distribute the family work equitably in all but the task area of child care.

Table 2: Mean Scores in the Four Task Areas of Wives and

Husbands with Similar and Dissimilar Employment Histories

Task Areas

		Meeting Each other's Psychological and Sexual Needs	Attending to the Mechanics of Living Together	Maintaining Relations with the Community	Raising Children
Employment History	Similar Employment History	Wife 7.72	Wife 6.64	Wife 7.64	Wife 8.75
		Husband 7.19	Husband 6.72	Husband 6.75	Husband 6.75
	Dissimilar Employment History	Wife 7.54	Wife 7.86	Wife 8.27	Wife 8.90
		Husband 7.19	Husband 4.94	Husband 5.92	Husband 4.83

DISCUSSION

The results of this study demonstrate that for this group of 32 professional couples, couples with a similar employment history distribute the family work more equitably than couples with a dissimilar employment history in the task areas of maintaining relations with the community—friends, neighbors, relatives, school personnel, and colleagues—and attending to the mechanics of family life, such as cooking, cleaning, shopping, and planning. There was no difference between SEH and DEH couples in the distribution of effort in the areas of meeting each other's psychological and sexual needs or in taking care of children. In the area of intimacy, all couples were mutually responsive to each other's needs, and in the area of parenthood, all wives did more child care than their husbands.

The findings of this study do not offer unequivocal support for the conclusions of either the questionnaire/interview or the time-budget studies. Some of the differences in findings can undoubtedly be attributed to the fact that the present study's sample is a professional one, as opposed to one of mixed occupational groups. However, differences in measurement strategies may also account for a large part of the discrepancies (Pleck, 1976). The questionnaire/interview studies measure relative proportions of work done by husbands and wives in a few task areas. The present study measured relative proportions of work done in an almost exhaustive array of task areas. Finally, the time-budget studies measure actual time spent in a few task categories.

In this study, there were no significant differences overall in the relative proportions of family work done by SEH and DEH wives, indicating that an increase from part- to full-time employment is not necessarily balanced by a decrease in family work. The time spent on tasks may well diminish, but not the number of task areas in which the wife does 50% or more of the work. This finding contradicts the questionnaire/interview data that show the woman's family work decreasing as her time spent in employed work increases. The finding of an overall increase in the husbands' proportion of family work associated with their wives' employment status—an increase due to the greater number of shared tasks for SEH than DEH couples, leading to an increase in SEH husbands' proportion of family work without an apparent decrease in SEH wives'—fits the questionnaire/interview but not the time-budget studies. Unfortunately, the discrepancies are difficult to resolve because of the two types of measurement differences:

task area comprehensiveness and proportional vs. absolute assessment of time spent in family work.

Future researchers interested in this topic would probably be advised to have couples respond to an exhaustive set of family tasks, as was attempted in this study. Whether proportional or absolute time measures are better indicators of a couple's experience of their division of labor has yet to be determined. Do couples weight type, quantity, and duration of family work in reckoning what will constitute an equitable or less than equitable division of labor? If the wife spends an hour each on five tedious tasks, will the couple feel that she has done her share of the week's work, given that her husband has spent eight hours doing the gardening he loves? Until we know more about the psychological meanings of various distributions of family work, researchers would do well to collect the couple's overall estimates of the degree of equity in their arrangements, as well as proportional and absolute time data.

The breakdown of the equitable distribution of tasks in the area of child care for the SEH couples is noteworthy. It seems to this researcher that only a complex interaction between husbands and wives can account for this phenomenon; an understanding of the wife or husband alone is not sufficient to explain the imbalance with which these couples live in this one task area.

Sex-role ideology is pervasive in our culture. Men and women, boys and girls all "know" what the culture deems appropriate behavior for each sex. Cultural prescriptions may be changing now, but the men and women in this sample grew up before the present wave of feminism, before Mr. Rogers's reassurance that it is fine for boys to cry and before Dr. Spock's (1976) conversion and assertion that it is a right and all right for mothers to work outside the home. The couples in this study "knew" a different code. Boys didn't play with dolls and men didn't take care of children, either in the home or on the job. Boys didn't learn how to cook, or sew, or clean, and men founded households without having daily householding skills. Since sex-role stereotyping exists for both child care and housekeeping, and since men haven't rehearsed either set of activities as boys, why should they more easily perform the one than the other as adults?

The answer, I think, comes from the fact that women have been subjected to complementary social conditioning. Moreover, the negative sanctions for deviations from convention in the area of child care are much more clearly spelled out than in the area of householding. Women who are poor cooks or sloppy housecleaners may be insulted or mocked, but there is no extensive literature documenting their faults or cultural consensus about the consequences. Bad mothers, on the other hand, are reviled, and popular wisdom as well as social-science studies have told women for decades that employed mothers *are* bad mothers. The harmful effects on children attributed to their mothers' employment include: breach of basic trust, emotional and cognitive deprivation, juvenile delinquency, diminished school performance, and faulty acquisition of sex-role identities (Hoffman, 1974; Howell, 1973; Howrigan, 1973). At some level, most mothers feel guilty about the time they spend away from their children. The time working women devote to child care can be viewed as a function of what they want to do and what they feel they ought to do.

Thus, couples negotiate with each other so that wives consciously or unconsciously take on the child-care tasks as a means of "compensation" for their hours away from home, and husbands work it out—again, not always consciously—so that the family work they do includes the tasks that are less threatening to their masculine selves. The children, too, may be a factor. Reacting to their perception of cultural expectations, they may differentially call upon their parents, insisting, for instance, that mother, not father, tuck them into bed. Until sex-role imagery legitimates male nurturance and various forms of female work, it is unlikely that couples will share child care equally.

REFERENCES

Atkinson, J. W. *Motives in fantasy, action, and society*. Princeton: Van Nostrand, 1958.
Bahr, S. J. Effects on power and division of labor. In L. Hoffman & F. I. Nye (Eds.), *Working mothers*. San Francisco: Jossey-Bass, 1974.
Duvall, E. M. *Family development*. New York: J. P. Lippincott, 1957.
Hess, R., & Handel, G. *Family worlds*. Chicago: University of Chicago Press, 1959.
Hoffman, L. Effects on child. In L. Hoffman & F. I. Nye (Eds.), *Working mothers*. San Francisco: Josey-Bass, 1974.
Holmstrom, L. L. *The two-career family*. Cambridge, Mass.: Schenkman, 1972.
Howell, M. C. Employed mothers and their families. *Pediatrics*, 1973, *52*, 252–263, 327–343.
Howrigan, G. *Effects of working mothers on children*. Cambridge, Mass.: Center for the Study of Public Policy, 1973.
Monthly Labor Review. Washington, D. C.: Department of Labor Statistics, November 1975.
Myrdal, A., & Klein, V. *Women's two roles: Home and work*. London: Routledge and Kegan Paul, 1956.
Pleck, J. H. Men's new roles in the family: Housework and child care. Ann Arbor: Institute for Social Research, University of Michigan, 1976.
Poloma, M. M., & Garland, T. N. The married professional woman: A study in the tolerance of domestication. *Journal of Marriage and the Family*, 1971b., *33*, 531–540.
Rapoport, R., & Rapoport, R. N. The dual-career family: A variant pattern. *Human Relations*, 1969, *22*, 3–30.

THE EMPLOYMENT PATTERN OF PROFESSIONAL COUPLES

Robinson, J. *How Americans use time: A social psychological analysis.* Forthcoming publication, (c.) 1977 by Praeger Publishers.
Safilios-Rothschild, C. The influence of wives' commitment upon some aspects of family organization and dynamics. *Journal of Marriage and the family,* 1970, *32,* 681–691.
Spock, Benjamin. *Baby and child care.* New York: Pocket Books, 1976.
Walker, K. Time spent by husbands in household work. *Family Economics Review,* June 1970, 8–11.

Determinants of Male Family-Role Performance

Carolyn C. Perrucci, Harry R. Potter, and Deborah L. Rhoads

Purdue University

Three competing hypotheses are tested regarding determinants of hus-band's (vs. wife's) participation in 12 selected household/child-care activi-ties. The research utilizes interview responses of husbands, although it com-pares responses of both husbands and wives in a proportionate stratified area-probability sample from adjacent midwestern cities. The socialization-ideology hypothesis receives the strongest, albeit modest, support of the three hypotheses. Only marginal support is found for the relative husband/ wife resources hypothesis, emphasizing professional employment of wives. No support is found for the time-availability hypothesis. Implications for the further integration of work and family roles for men are considered.

Although recent theoretical writing about the family has em-phasized an increasing integration of work and family roles for both sexes (Fogarty, Rapoport, & Rapoport, 1971; Rapoport & Rapoport, 1971), empirical studies have left open to question the extent as well as determinants of married men's participation in household and child-care activities (Pleck, 1977). More specifically, from the 1920s to the present, married women typically have performed a full week (50+ hours) of household work, although employed married women now spend only about half the time in housework as their unem-

---

The authors are affiliated with the Department of Sociology and Anthropology, Stone Hall, Purdue University, West Lafayette, Indiana 47907. They are grateful for the help received from Brent Smith, who provided computer-programming assistance for this study. Requests for reprints should be sent to Dr. Carolyn C. Perrucci.

0361-6843/78/1500-0053$00.95 © 1978 Human Sciences Press

DETERMINANTS OF MALE FAMILY-ROLE PERFORMANCE

ployed peers (Vanek, 1974). The literature also clearly documents that married women, including mothers of young children, have been increasingly participating in the labor force (Waite, 1976; Waldman, 1970). With respect to married men, on the other hand, trend data indicate that their labor-force participation rates have been relatively full and constant over time (Ferriss, 1971), whereas the amount of household work performed has been relatively small (Blood & Wolfe, 1960; Bryson, Bryson, Licht, & Licht, 1976; Farkas, 1976; Stafford, Backman, & Dibona, 1977) and constant over time (Duncan, Schuman, & Duncan, 1973).

Husbands' family-role performance may very well be limited in comparison to that of wives in the aggregate, but individual variation in husband's family time exists and is of at least equal theoretical significance. The present study aims to extend extant research by examining determinants of husbands' (vs. wives') participation in 12 selected household/child-care activities. In doing so the study tests three competing hypotheses in the area: (1) the relative husband/wife resources hypothesis (Bahr, 1972; Blood & Wolfe, 1960; Stafford et al., 1977), (2) the subcultural or socialization hypothesis regarding values and ideology (Stafford et al., 1977), and (3) the time-available hypothesis (Stafford et al., 1977). The research is also innovative because it utilizes responses of husbands as the dependent variable although it compares responses of both husbands and wives.

According to the relative-resource hypothesis, husbands and wives command in their marriage a certain level of a variety of resources, including education and occupational prestige. (Although income is unquestionably a resource, its effects are usually ascertained under the rubric of yet a fourth "economic" hypothesis that posits that both husbands and wives divide up their time between marketwork, housework, and leisure, and that their decision is based upon a comparison of the husband's and wife's efficiency in both marketwork (i.e., relative wage rates) and housework. A recent study by Farkas (1976) finds no effect of husband/wife relative wage rates on the number of hours of housework performed by husbands. While such data are available in this study, they are not included because of the small number (51) of employed women.) The above-mentioned resources are power resources, and the spouse who controls the relatively greater share can presumably minimize his/her participation in undesired activities, including household work/childcare. If, with increases in the husband's educational level or occupational prestige, he does less housework (holding constant the wife's educational or occupational level), the relative-resources hypothesis is supported.

CAROLYN C. PERRUCCI, HARRY R. POTTER, DEBORAH L. RHOADS

Research evidence for this hypothesis is inconclusive at this time (Blood & Wolfe, 1960; Farkas, 1976; Stafford et al., 1977; Hesselbart, 1976).

The socialization-ideology hypothesis posits that the household division of labor depends upon the nature of sex-role ideology acquired by women and men as children and/or adults. According to a rather traditional sex-role ideology, household work and child care have been considered to be the major role of married women, not men (Bem, 1970; Poloma & Garland, 1971). An egalitarian sex-role ideology, on the other hand, should be predictive of husband/wife household task sharing, regardless of power and authority considerations. A study of a small sample of married male college students found that time spent on performance of household tasks was less if their "ideal" partner, their reasons for marriage, the parental household division of labor, as well as men's current sex-role ideology were traditional (Stafford et al., 1977). Moreover, a national study of households (Farkas, 1976) found that low education of husband was associated with fewer hours of housework performed by him, whereas high education was associated with more housework. It was unclear from this study whether or not high education reflected a male ideology for egalitarian behavior. A study of Floridian couples, however, showed that both husband's education and his attitude toward women's equality affected the extent to which he shared household tasks with his wife (Hesselbart, 1976). Specifically, the higher the husband's education and the less opposed he was to women's equality, the more he shared tasks.

According to the time-available hypothesis, husbands and wives allocate household tasks and child care on the basis of time available to each spouse for such activities. Employment of the wife has been assumed to lessen her availability for the unpaid activities, and evidence has shown that employed wives spend less time doing housework than unemployed wives (Vanek, 1974). Data regarding the effect of wife employment on husband's participation, however, are conflicting. Blood and Hamblin (1958), Blood and Wolfe (1960), Hoffman (1960), Layne and Lowe (1977), and Safilios-Rothschild (1970) reported that the husband assumed a greater share of the housework if his wife was employed. A Greek study (Safilios-Rothschild, 1970) found that husbands participated more rarely and in fewer activities if their wives had high rather than low work commitment (i.e., accorded a high degree of importance to their work and would work regardless of financial need). Use of hired help, however, was more characteristic of wives with high, rather than low, com-

DETERMINANTS OF MALE FAMILY-ROLE PERFORMANCE

mitment. On the other hand, Hesselbart (1976), Stafford et al. (1977), and Bryson et al. (1976) found that wife's employment was unrelated to husband's housework, although it led to greater use of commercial services (Nolan, 1963) and paid nonfamily help (Bryson et al., 1976). Powell (1963) discovered that when the oldest child was an adolescent, rather than younger, the husbands of employed women participated in fewer home activities than did the husbands of nonemployed wives.

The number of children in the home is another variable that is assumed to lessen married women's time available for housework, but empirical evidence for this is inconclusive. Farkas (1976) and Campbell (1970) reported that husbands helped increasingly with household tasks with the presence (vs. absence) of children and as number of children increased, respectively. Marital duration and husband's age, which may reflect family size and/or age of children, were found to be inversely related to husband's task participation by Blood and Wolfe (1960) and Silverman and Hill (1967), and by Olsen (1960), respectively. Controlling for the presence of a preschool-age child, however, Hesselbart (1976) found no effect of marital duration on spouse task sharing. Layne and Lowe (1977), moreover, have shown that as parity or child-spacing intervals increased, both mothers and fathers reallocated some child-care and cooking tasks to other family members (usually older children) but not to each other.

METHODS

Data for this study were from the adjacent cities of Lafayette and West Lafayette, Indiana and were obtained by personal interviews in May 1972. A proportionate stratified-area probability sample was used, with census blocks placed in four strata on the basis of owned-housing value, which served as an indicator of social class. Twenty-eight blocks were selected, with a random starting point designated for each block. Interviewers attempted to contact every third house. The interviewers worked in two-person teams (five female-male; four male-male). Interviews were done concurrently, but independently, with the husband and the wife. Interviews were completed with 98 couples; there were an additional 30 households in the sample where no one was home or it was not possible to schedule an interview before the end of the data-collection phase.

The dependent variable, husband's role performance, was based on the husband's response to how he and his wife shared 12 household activities. The activities were listed in terms of who (1) did the grocery shopping, (2) got husband's breakfast on work days, (3) straightened living room when company was coming, (4) mowed the lawn, (5) shoveled the sidewalk, (6) did the evening dishes, (7) repaired things around the house, (8) kept track of the money and bills, (9) was responsible for getting the car repaired, (10) was responsible for taking care of the children when they were sick, (11) bought the children's clothes, and (12) did the driving when traveling together. Response categories for each of the activities were (1) husband always, (2) husband more than wife, (3) husband and wife equally, (4) wife more than husband, (5) wife always, and (6) not applicable.

While the central focus of this paper is on husband's task performance, it is important to compare *his* responses with *his wife's* responses on his performance, particularly in view of the discrepancies reported on this issue (Scanzoni, 1965; Safilios-Rothschild, 1969). Husbands reported that they did these tasks more than their wives reported they did. Of the 12 activities, husbands said they did 6.4 activities (standard deviation 1.5) equally or more than their wives. Wives, however, said their husbands did only 5.9 (standard deviation 1.6) activities. The difference between the means is significant ($t=2.24$, $p \leqslant .05$, two-tailed test).

The specific measure used here asked who did each activity, with the response categories shown above. The score was obtained by counting the number of activities the husband said that he did *equally* or *more* than his wife, divided by the total number of items minus those that were not applicable, i.e., 12 − number of not applicable activities. Activities involving lawns, sidewalks, and children were "not applicable" for as many as about one-third of the respondents. Succinctly, the dependent variable was the proportion of applicable activities the husband said he did equally or more often than his wife. This measure had substantial differentiation, with a range from .36 to 1, mean = .59, and standard deviation = .14, as shown in Table 1.

The predictor variables were placed in three broad categories for the purpose of describing them: those relating to ideology or belief about the family, those related to resources available, and those affecting time availability. The ideology indicators included eight Likert-type attitude items with five responses from strongly agree to strongly disagree. These are listed verbatim as the first eight items under "Ideology" in Table 1. Consideration was given to creating a composite score, but the interitem correlations were too low, with only one exceeding .50. It was felt that it would be preferable, therefore, to use each item separately. Although some of the items appeared to have related content, such as power or traditional roles, under conditions of social change there may be quite differential rates of change in ideology across specific issues, thus contributing to the apparent lack of a common underlying dimension. Three additional ideology indicators were whether the husband's mother worked, scored dichotomously (0=No, 1=Yes); the husband's rating of his marital happiness on a five-point scale (1=much happier, 5=much less happy); and the husband's preference to engage in leisure time activities with his wife (1 = "all the time," 5 = "never)."

The resources variables included husband's and wife's education (eight

DETERMINANTS OF MALE FAMILY-ROLE PERFORMANCE

Table 1

Means and Standard Deviations for All Variables in Regression Analysis of

Husband's Family Role Performance.

	Mean	Standard deviation
Dependent Variable		
Husband's role performance	.59	.14
Independent Variables[a]		
Ideology		
Young children need to be with their mother more than their father.	2.66	1.04
A working woman should still be primarily responsible for taking care of the house and the children.	2.78	1.04
A pre-school child is likely to suffer emotional damage if his or her mother works.	2.97	1.15
Nature intended women to be homemakers and men to be workers.	3.04	1.13
In cases of disagreement within the marriage, the husband should have the final say.	3.46	1.05
Normally, a son should receive more education than a daughter.	3.22	1.16
A stable family must have a dominant father.	3.09	1.01
Women should work only if it is financially necessary.	3.39	1.10
Husband's mother worked	.41	.49
Husband's marital happiness	1.89	.77
Husband prefers to engage in leisure activities with wife.	2.26	.78
Resources		
Husband's education	5.15	1.92
Husband's occupation	4.41	2.77
Wife's education	4.57	1.52
Wife: housewife[b]	.45	.50
Wife works: non-professional[b]	.42	.50
Husband expects wife to be working full-time outside the home during next ten years	2.03	.91
Time availability		
Number of children at home	1.80	1.55
Marital duration	12.92	10.16
Husband's age	36.50	11.60

Note: Sample size drops to 74 in the regression analysis because of missing data.

[a] Underline indicates abbreviated variable names used in Table 2.

[b] Dummy variables

categories from less than seven years to postgraduate MA or PhD); husband's occupation, coded as a modified version of the Edwards occupational scale expanded to 12 categories, with low scores assigned to higher status occupations; and wife's occupation, treated as three dummy variables: (1) housewife, (2) nonprofessional occupation, and (3) professional occupation. One other resource variable was whether the husband expected his wife to be employed full-time outside the house during the next 10 years (1=yes, 2=no, part-time work, 3=no).

Three different aspects of time were measured. One was the number of children currently living in the household (actual number coded with 8 = 8 or more). The second was length of marriage, in years, and last was husband's age in years.

RESULTS

As indicated above, three possible hypotheses for the division of household/child care labor among married couples are under consideration: (1) relative resources, (2) socialization-ideology, and (3) time availability. The initial comparison of these hypotheses was done by examining the zero-order correlation coefficients between the predictor variables and husband's task performance. These coefficients are generally low, with only two being statistically significant at $p \le .05$ and in the predicted direction. Both of these are ideology items: "A stable family must have a dominant father," $r=.34$; and "Nature intended women to be homemakers and men to be workers," $r=.24$. A third, time-availability variable, number of children at home, has the next largest coefficient, but it is in the opposite direction of that predicted and thus does not support the time-availability hypothesis. Thus, initially it appears that the socialization-ideology hypothesis offers more of an explanation for husband's task performance than either of the other two hypotheses.

Next, the set of variables associated with each hypothesis was examined separately. Again, the ideology variables clearly have a stronger relationship to husband's task performance than either the resources or time-availability variables. The multiple-correlation coefficient for the set of ideology variables (entered in step-wise regression order) is .47 (significant at $p \le .01$) for six variables. "A stable family must have a dominant father" is the strongest predictor among the ideology variables. None of the time-availability variables is related as predicted to husband's task performance. The multiple-correlation coefficient (.22; $p > .05$) for the three variables is not

DETERMINANTS OF MALE FAMILY-ROLE PERFORMANCE

significant. Virtually all of this coefficient is accounted for by number of children at home, which, contrary to the hypothesis, is inversely related to husband's task performance. The resource variables, considered as a set by themselves, are not significantly related to husband's task performance; this holds for the multiple correlation (.32; p> .05) as well as each of the variables individually.

In order to further assess each hypothesis, the measure of husband's family-role performance was regressed on all of the independent variables in the study. Table 2 lists the independent variables in the order they entered the step-wise multiple-regression equation,

Table 2

Regression Analysis of Husband's Family Role Performance

Independent Variables	Standardized Regression Coefficient	Predictor Signif- icance	Multiple R	Multiple R Signif- icance
Stable family (I)	.381	.01	.34	.01
Wife: housewife[a] (R)	-.415	.07	.38	.01
Work financially necessary (I)	-.402	.01	.43	.01
Husband's education (R)	.400	.07	.48	.01
Husband's occupation (R)	.302	.09	.53	.01
Women homemakers (I)	.202	.22	.55	.01
Prefer leisure with wife (I)	-.080	.56	.57	.01
Number of children (A)	-.111	.41	.57	.01
Working woman care house (I)	.084	.51	.58	.01
Children need mother (I)	-.131	.36	.59	.01
Husband final say (I)	.129	.33	.60	.01
Wife: non-professional[a] (R)	-.187	.40	.60	.01
Wife's education (R)	-.141	.48	.60	.01
Marital duration (A)	-.370	.17	.61	.01
Husband's age (A)	.337	.22	.62	.01
Husband's mother worked (I)	.074	.57	.62	.01
Wife to be working (R)	.056	.65	.63	.02
Pre-school child suffer (I)	-.028	.83	.63	.03
Son more education (I)	.025	.85	.63	.04
Marital happiness (I)	-.013	.92	.63	.06

Note: Sample size drops to 74 because of missing data.
Catagories of predictor variables are designated as follows: ideology (I); relative resources (R); and availability (A).

[a] Dummy variables

CAROLYN C. PERRUCCI, HARRY R. POTTER, DEBORAH L. RHOADS

shows the standardized regression coefficients and significance level for each independent variable when all variables are in the equation, and shows the cumulative multiple R and its significance for each successive independent variable.

This analysis procedure allows us to examine (1) the order in which each independent variable is added to the regression equation and (2) how much variance is explained by each additional variable. Looking at the ordering of variables, there is no clear pattern of any one set of variables predominating in sequence. The first variable to enter is a socialization-ideology variable; however, three of the first five are resource variables; and a time-availability variable enters only eighth. The multiple correlation is significant through 16 ($p \leqslant .01$) or 19 ($p \leqslant .05$) variables with R being .62 or .63, respectively. Only the first 16 variables are considered as statistically significant in the remainder of the paper. Of these 16 variables, eight are socialization (of a possible 11), five are resource variables (out of six), and three (out of three) are time-availability variables. Although wife's occupation is a single variable in terms of subjects' responses, it was treated as a dummy variable in this analysis; two of the categories were entered as dummy variates, resulting in six, rather than five, predictor variables. The third response category, wife employed in a professional occupation, served as the residual (cf. Blalock, 1972). The remaining four variables, including one resource and three ideology measures, are not statistically significant at the .01 level and add very little to the multiple correlation.

Socialization-Ideology Hypothesis

To more adequately assess the three theoretical perspectives, it is useful to examine the variables within each perspective directly. The two statistically significant ($p = \leqslant .01$) variables in the regression equation are ideology variables. Specifically, the greater the husband's disagreement with the attitude "A stable family must have a dominant father," the more household/childcare activities he participates in. The husband's response to another marital-power ideology item, "In cases of disagreement within the marriage, the husband should have the final say," is also related in the same direction to his task participation in the home. In contrast, agreement (rather than disagreement) with "Women should work only if it is financially necessary" is significantly related to greater male family-role performance. In addition, the greater the husband's disagreement with "Nature intended women to be homemakers and men to be workers" and "A working woman should still be primarily responsible for taking care of the house and the children," the more he participates in home activities, which is consistent with the socialization-ideology hypothesis; that is, the less traditional the husband's ideology regarding women's home and (paid) work roles, the more activities in which he participates. However, the opposite is found with regard to "Young children need to be with their mother more than their father"; here, the greater the agreement, the greater the husband's participation.

Another ideology variable in the regression equation concerns the extent to which husbands prefer to engage in their leisure-time activities with their wives. Since both husbands and wives are assumed here to allocate their time between paid work, unpaid home work/childcare, and leisure, it is expected that (controlling for participation in paid-work roles) husbands who prefer to share leisure activities with their wives will also share home tasks with their spouses. Although the effect of such leisure preferences is not individually statistically significant for our sample of husbands, the direction of effect is consistent with the hypothesis and adds significantly to the multiple correlation.

Employment (vs. nonemployment) of the husband's mother could affect his ideology and behavior (i.e., make him less traditional), especially if such employment were related to more task participation by husband's father (Stafford et al., 1977). In our sample, mother's employment is not individually significantly related to son's family-role performance but does contribute significantly to the multiple correlation, and the direction of effect is consistent with the socialization-ideology hypothesis.

Happiness in a marital relationship could influence a husband to participate with his wife in household/child-care activities, irrespective of other considerations (Farkas, 1976). Husband's perception of the happiness of his marriage relative to that of other couples is not significantly related to husband's role performance in this study. In addition, two other ideology items, "A preschool child is likely to suffer emotional damage if his or her mother works" and "Normally a son should receive more education than a daughter" are not significant, either.

Relative-Resources Hypothesis

The most important of the relative-resources variables is whether the wife is a housewife or professionally employed, which enters the

CAROLYN C. PERRUCCI, HARRY R. POTTER, DEBORAH L. RHOADS

regression equation second. Although the regression coefficient is not individually significant, it indicates husbands whose wives are not employed do 12% fewer tasks than those whose wives are professionally employed. This is consistent with the relative-resource hypothesis. Similarly, husband's education and occupation and wife's education also are not individually significant, although the multiple correlation is significant when they are included. The regression coefficient for "wife: nonprofessional" is not even marginally significant individually, and it adds very little to R, even though it is among the first 16 variables. One resource variable, "Husband expects wife to be working full-time outside the home during the next 10 years," is not significant and adds little to the regression equation.

Time-Availability Hypothesis

None of the three variables pertaining to availability of time is significantly related to husband's family-role performance, once other variables are controlled. Although the multiple correlation including all three of these variables is significant, it does not add a great deal to the coefficient. Number of children at home, which enters the regression equation eighth, appears to be the most important predictor of husband's task performance, although again not in the expected direction. Length of marriage and age of husband are not individually related to the dependent variable, although they enter the regression equation *14th* and *15th*.

SUMMARY AND CONCLUSIONS

The purpose of this study was to compare three different theoretical explanations for variations in husband's family/household task performance currently in the literature on the family. Multiple indicators were used for each theoretical perspective. The socialization-ideology hypothesis, that is, that husband's performance behavior results from an acquired belief that he should or should not assist with household tasks, received the strongest support of the three. That support was only modest, at best, however, since only two of the indicators had statistically significant zero-order relationships with task performance. When the effects of *all* other variables were partialed out in multiple-regression analysis, one of these indicators was no longer significant, but a third ideology indicator became significant, although the direction of its relationship was the opposite of that expected.

DETERMINANTS OF MALE FAMILY-ROLE PERFORMANCE

The comparative strength of the socialization-ideology hypothesis was seen when the indicators associated with each hypothesis were run in a multiple regression with husband's task performance. Here, of the three sets of indicators, only the multiple-correlation coefficient for the socialization indicators was statistically significant.

Only marginal support was found for the relative-resources hypothesis, which says that the spouse with the more resources will perform fewer household tasks. None of the relative-resources indicators was significant initially; however, in the multiple-correlation analysis, wives' being professionally employed rather than housewives was related to husband's performance, as was husband's education and occupation and wife's education. There was no support for the time-availability hypothesis. One of its indicators was the eighth variable to enter the step-wise multiple-regression equation, but the finding was that the greater the number of children in the household, the less the husband did, which was the opposite of what was expected.

The present study was not specifically directed toward investigation of the dual-career family, the theme of this journal issue; however, it focused on one aspect of family activity that may inhibit or facilitate wife participation in a career. This aspect is husband's degree of participation in housework/child-care activities, which is commonly viewed as a way to reduce work overload for wives and, hence, affect their occupational achievement (Fogarty et al., 1971; Miller, 1971).

An implication of these findings is that further integration of work and family roles for men depends substantially on socialization experiences that foster an ideology or belief that is consonant with sharing household/child-care tasks. Sharing may mean that the man does a substantial portion of the tasks himself or that he shares them equally with his spouse. Formal education may be one such socialization experience; for example, the zero-order correlations between husband's education on the one hand and the "Stable family must have a dominant father," "Nature intended women to be homemakers," and "Women should work only if it is financially necessary" ideology items on the other hand are .30, .55, and .50, respectively ($df = 72$, $p < .05$ for all). Highly educated men are also more likely than less educated men to be married to women of relatively high education ($r = .68$), who, in turn, are more likely than less educated wives to endorse an egalitarian ideology. As Miller (1971) has noted, the relative egalitarianism of husband/wife roles depends, in part at least, on wives' willingness to share what in our culture is

CAROLYN C. PERRUCCI, HARRY R. POTTER, DEBORAH L. RHOADS

generally considered to be women's traditional role in the home. Additionally, highly educated men are more likely than their less educated peers to hold high-prestige occupations (−.69). Pleck (1977) suggests that ultimately it will be ability to modify institutional work-role constraints that will permit greater participation in the home if men so desire (i.e., given an egalitarian ideology). It is possible that the necessary flexibility in institutional work-role constraints may be at least partially related to occupational prestige. It remains an important task of future research to investigate in even greater depth the effects that husbands' ideologies and resources have on family-role performance.

REFERENCES

Bahr, S. J. Comment on the study of family power structure: A review 1960–1969. *Journal of Marriage and the Family*, 1972, *34*, 239–243.

Bem, D. J. *Beliefs, attitudes and human affairs.* Belmont, Calif.: Brooks/Cole, 1970.

Blalock, H. M. Jr. *Social statistics.* New York: McGraw-Hill, 1972.

Blood, R., & Hamblin, R. The effects of the wife's employment on the family power structure. *Social Forces*, 1958, *36*, 347–352.

Blood, R., & Wolfe, D. *Husbands and wives.* New York: The Free Press, 1960.

Bryson, R. B., Bryson, J. B., Licht, M. H., & Licht, B. G. The professional pair: Husband and wife psychologists. *American Psychologist*, 1976, *31*, 10–16.

Campbell, F. Family growth and variation in family role structure. *Journal of Marriage and the Family*, 1970, *32*, 45–52.

Duncan, O., Schuman, H., & Duncan, B. *Social change in a metropolitan community.* New York: Russell Sage Foundation, 1973.

Farkas, G. Education, wage rates and the division of labor between husband and wife. *Journal of Marriage and the Family*, 1976, *38*, 473–483.

Ferriss, A. *Indicators of trends in the status of american women.* New York: Russell Sage Foundation, 1971.

Fogarty, M. P., Rapoport, R., & Rapoport, R. N. *Sex, career and family.* London: Allen and Unwin, 1971.

Hesselbart, S. *Does charity begin at home? Attitudes toward women, household tasks, and household decision-making.* Paper presented at the meeting of the American Sociological Association, New York City, August 1976.

Hoffman, L. W. Effects of the employment of mothers on parental power relations and the division of household tasks. *Marriage and Family Living*, 1960, *22*, 27–35.

Layne, N. R., Jr., & Lowe, J. The effects of the timing of successive births upon the social organization of American families. *Sociological Focus*, 1977, *10*, 89–96.

Miller, S. M. On men: The making of a confused middle-class husband. *Social Policy*, 1971, *2*, 33–39.

Nolan, F. L. Rural employment and husbands and wives. In F. I. Nye & L. W. Hoffman (Eds.), *The employed mother in America.* Chicago: Rand McNally, 1963.

Olsen, M. E. Distribution of family responsibilities and social stratification. *Journal of Marriage and the Family*, 1960, *22*, 60–65.

Pleck, J., The work-family role-system. *Social Problems*, 1977, *24*, 417–427.

Poloma, M., & Garland, N. The married professional woman: A study in the tolerance of domestication. *Journal of Marriage and the Family*, 1971, *33*, 531–540.

DETERMINANTS OF MALE FAMILY-ROLE PERFORMANCE

Powell, K. S. Family variables. In F. I. Nye & L. W. Hoffman (Eds.), *The employed mother in America.* Chicago: Rand McNally, 1963.

Rapoport, R., & Rapoport, R. *Dual career families.* Middlesex, England: Penguin Books, 1971.

Safilios-Rothschild, C. Family sociology or wives' family sociology? A cross-cultural examination of decision-making. *Journal of Marriage and the Family,* 1969, *31,* 290–301.

Safilios-Rothschild, C. The influence of the wife's degree of work commitment upon some aspects of family organization and dynamics. *Journal of Marriage and the Family,* 1970, *32,* 681–691.

Scanzoni, J. A note on the sufficiency of wife responses in family research. *Pacific Sociological Review,* 1965, *8,* 109–115.

Silverman, W., & Hill, R. Task allocation in marriage in the United States and Belgium. *Journal of Marriage and the Family,* 1967, *29,* 353–359.

Stafford, R., Backman, E., & Dibona, P. The division of labor among cohabiting and married couples. *Journal of Marriage and the Family,* 1977, *39,* 43–57.

Vanek, J. Time spent in housework. *Scientific American,* 1974, *231,* 116–120.

Waite, L. J. Working wives: 1940–1960. *American Sociological Review,* 1976, *41,* 65–80.

Waldman, E. Women at work: Changes in the labor force activity of women. *Monthly Labor Review,* 1970, *93,* 10–18.

Family Size, Satisfaction, and Productivity in Dual-Career Couples

Rebecca Bryson, Jeff B. Bryson, and Marilyn F. Johnson

San Diego State University

Responses by 196 couples—in which both spouses were members of the American Psychological Association—to a series of questions regarding domestic satisfaction, job satisfaction, and productivity were examined as a function of years since final degree and number of children in the family. There were consistent differences between the sexes in responses to these questions, indicating that wives were less satisfied and less productive than husbands in these couples. However, prior differences between groups in age, years since final degree, and rate of full-time employment disallowed any meaningful interpretations of these differences. Family size was found to influence satisfaction with time available for domestic activities, job, and avocations. Significant interactions indicated that these effects were more severe for the wife than for the husband, indicating that wives in dual-career couples bear a disproportionate share of the burden for child care. Influences of family size on satisfaction with rate of advancement and freedom to set long-term career goals were also noted.

Prior research on wives' employment outside the home has revealed a subtle but pervasive bias regarding the relative importance of the wife's employment. In virtually all studies, the principal independent variable has been work status, i.e., whether the wife is employed or not. Groups of working wives are compared with those not employed outside the home in an effort to detect differences in such variables as marital satisfaction, adjustment of children, or mental health of the wife as a function of paid outside employment.

Marilyn Johnson is now at the University of Minnesota. Requests for reprints should be sent to Rebecca Bryson, Department of Psychology, San Diego State University, San Diego, California 92182.

FAMILY SIZE, SATISFACTION, AND PRODUCTIVITY IN DUAL-CAREER COUPLES

The comparison of employed and nonemployed wives is consistent with the assumption that the wife's major dilemma concerns the choice of whether or not she should obtain outside employment, especially when there are children in the family unit. That is, being married and having children are variables over which she has relatively little control given that she is married, while seeking outside employment is an option that may or may not be exercised. However, an increasingly common dilemma today, particularly in couples where both husband and wife have received professional training, is not whether or not to work but whether or not to have children, or how many children to have. That is, wives in these couples are committed to relatively continuous professional employment and are concerned with the effects of childbearing on both domestic and job-related satisfaction and productivity.

A second aspect of this biased expectation regarding the "wife's dilemma" is that relatively little attention has been given to the effects of number of children on the husband's job performance and sources of satisfaction or dissatisfaction, ignoring the possibility that the husband in dual-career couples may also feel increasing demands or may change the nature of his participation in the family unit as family size increases. While the presence of children may have little influence on the husband's job performance or satisfaction in "traditional" families, it may be that husbands in dual-career families are more likely to share responsibilities for childrearing, increasing the total demands on their time, a change that may be reflected in both domestic and job-related satisfaction as well as in job performance.

While data comparing employed and nonemployed wives do not provide information directly related to the choices faced by a dual-career family, they may be of some interest in making these decisions. Hoffman and Nye (1974) provide an excellent, carefully qualified review of research in this area. However, the results of these various research endeavors make one point rather clear: The effects of maternal employment are neither consistently good nor bad; rather, it depends upon the particular dependent variable examined. Adjustment, delinquency rates, and academic achievement of children, divorce rates and expressed marital satisfaction of husband and wife, and anxiety, self-concept, and likelihood of mental illness of the wife are not related in any simple way to the question of whether or not she works. Instead, outcomes on these variables appear to be a complex function of other factors, including the wife's motive for working, her educational level, the type of job in which she is employed, the quality of care the children receive from external sources,

REBECCA BRYSON, JEFF B. BRYSON, MARILYN F. JOHNSON

and her family's attitude toward her employment. Without knowledge of these factors the effects of maternal employment are difficult
to assess. When this is compounded by the emergence of a radically
new form of relationship, the dual-career couple, which requires a
different perspective in even asking the questions, such assessments
are impossible.

The present study employs the perspective that is more appropriate to the requirements of the dual-career couple: How does
number of children in the family affect job satisfaction, domestic
satisfaction, and productivity of both wife and husband? In order to
avoid many sources of confounding (although admittedly limiting the
generalizability of results), comparisons are limited to a single occupational group: couples in which both spouses are psychologists.

METHOD

Subjects

A sample of 196 couples who received husband/wife credit for mem-
bership in the American Psychological Association and who responded to
three extensive questionnaires designed by the authors provided data that
could be used in the analyses described in this paper (omissions on
one or more of the relevant variables altered the size of this sample available
for various analyses). The initial 196 couples represent approximately 33%
of those to whom questionnaires had been sent.

Questionnaires

Three questionnaires, one to be completed by the husband, another by
the wife, and a third to be completed by husband and wife jointly, were
constructed and sent out as a part of a larger study (Bryson, Bryson, Licht,
and Licht, 1976). Questions particularly pertinent to the present study included four questions on domestic satisfaction, six questions on job satisfaction, and two measures of productivity, in addition to questions concerning
number of children and years since final degree.

RESULTS

An overview of the relationship between family size (number of
children) and various demographic characteristics of our sample is
presented in Table 1. As may be seen, the median age for husbands

FAMILY SIZE, SATISFACTION, AND PRODUCTIVITY IN DUAL-CAREER COUPLES

Table 1.

Demographic Information

Number (%) of couples	47 (24)	36 (18)	62 (32)	51 (26)
Median Age				
Husband	37.4	40.0	44.0	48.7
Wife	35.8	35.5	41.2	44.7
Percent Ph.D.				
Husband	91.5	80.6	95.2	92.2
Wife	89.4	69.4	83.9	72.5
Current Employment Status				
Husband				
%fulltime	91.3	94.4	95.2	92.2
%parttime	4.3	2.8	4.8	3.9
%unemployed	4.4	2.8	0.0	3.9
Wife				
%fulltime	84.8	52.8	63.9	48.0
%parttime	10.9	25.5	26.2	42.0
%unemployed	4.3	22.2	9.8	10.0
Median annual income (in thousands)				
Husband	18.2	16.4	21.7	22.3
Wife	15.3	12.0	15.4	13.0

was consistently older than that of the wives, across all family sizes, with the difference ranging from less than two years (those with no children) to 4.5 years (those with one child). Husbands were also consistently more likely to have obtained a doctoral degree, and the discrepancy in PhD completion rate was related to the number of children, ranging from a difference of 2.1% among those with no children to a difference of 19.7% among those with three or more children. The PhD completion rate was, inexplicably, lowest for both husbands and wives with one child.

Number of children was also related to differences in current employment status. For husbands, there was no noticeable relationship between number of children and percent of full-time employment, with an average of approximately 98% of all husbands employed full-time. However, for wives, rate of employment was clearly influenced by number of children. Among those with no children, 84.8% were employed full-time; those with one or more children were employed full-time at a much lower rate, dropping to 48% among those with three or more children. The rate of part-time employment was also directly related to number of children, ranging from 10.9% for those with no children to 42% among those with three or more children. Again, there was an anomaly for those with only one child; wives in this group were the most likely to have been unemployed at the time of our survey, possibly reflecting a greater incidence of preschool children in this group, with a concomitant tendency for wives to elect to remain out of the labor market during that period.

It is also interesting to note that income increased across family size (and, of course, age) for the husbands but did not for the wives. For wives, the best correlate of median income is the percent currently employed full-time.

In general, these basic demographic characteristics demonstrate that childbearing has its greatest effect upon the employment status of the wife. Husbands are relatively unaffected, in terms of rate of employment or median income, by the number of children in the family. However, these analyses do not indicate how our respondents feel about their current employment status. For answers to these questions, we must turn to analyses of responses to questions regarding satisfaction with home and job.

The relationship between age and number of children made it necessary for us to control for age in our subsequent analyses. For this reason we divided respondents into three categories on the basis of age (actually, years since final degree, a measure of "employment age"), in addition to dividing them in terms of sex and number of children. All of the following analyses therefore employ a 2 (sex of respondent) X 4 (number of children) X 3 (years since final degree) design.

Domestic Satisfaction

One part of our questionnaire concerned questions regarding the respondents' satisfaction with domestic and nonemployment-related activities. The four questions reported here were:

(1) Are you satisfied with the amount of time you have for domestic activities?

(2) To what extent are you as a couple confronted with disagreements over division of labor at home?

(3) Are you satisfied with the amount of time you have for avocational activities?

(4) Are you satisfied with the amount of time you have to spend with your family?

In each case larger values imply greater dissatisfaction.

On the first question there was a significant main effect of sex [F $(1,366) = 145.6, p < .001$], indicating that wives (m = 1.91) were much less satisfied than husbands (m = 1.19) regarding the amount of time they had for domestic activities. There was also a significant main effect for number of children [F$(3,366) = 11.29, p < .001$], with those having more children being less satisfied (M = 1.31, 1.60, 1.65, and 1.65, for 0, 1, 2, and 3+ children, respectively). In addition, there was a significant sex-by-number-of-children interaction [F$(3,366) = 6.31, p < .001$], indicating that the difference between husbands' and wives' satisfaction with this item increased as family size increased; wives were increasingly dissatisfied with the amount of time that they had for domestic activities as number of children increased, while husbands' satisfaction with this aspect of domestic life was not related to number of children.

An analysis of factors that contribute to disagreements concerning division of labor indicated that only age, or years since final degree, was related to this source of discord in the family [F$(2,366) = 6.87, p < .01$]; those who had more recently obtained the PhD were more likely to report this as a problem. Although it might be presumed that increases in family size would be associated with increasing demands on time for performance of domestic activities, number of children was not related to disagreements over division of labor.

There was also a sex difference in satisfaction with the amount of time available for avocational activities [F$(1,336) = 6.66, p < .01$], with wives (m = 2.30) expressing more dissatisfaction than husbands (M = 1.65). There was also a marginally significant [F$(3,336) = 2.15, p < .10$] relationship between satisfaction and number of children, with satisfaction decreasing with number of children (M = 1.83, 1.79, 2.15, and 2.03, for those with 0, 1, 2, and 3+ children, respectively). As with satisfaction regarding time for domestic activities, there was an interaction between sex and number of children, with wives becoming increasingly dissatisfied as number of children increased while husbands' satisfaction was not related to number of children [F$(6,336) = 2.23, p < .05$].

On the final domestic-satisfaction question, regarding time available to spend with the family, there was only a marginally significant main effect of number of children [F$(3,336) = 2.12, p < .10$], with those having more children expressing somewhat greater problems in this area.

REBECCA BRYSON, JEFF B. BRYSON, MARILYN F. JOHNSON

Job-Related Satisfaction

Six separate questions regarding job-related satisfaction were analyzed as a part of this study. These questions were:
(1) Have you experienced career-development problems stemming from differential achievement of yourself and your spouse?
(2) Are you satisfied with your rate of professional advancement?
(3) Are you satisfied with your opportunity to interact with colleagues?
(4) Are you satisfied with your freedom to pursue long-range job goals?
(5) Are you satisfied with the regard your colleagues show for you?
(6) Are you satisfied with the time you have for professional activities?

Again, larger values are associated with greater dissatisfaction.

Wives (M = .34) were more likely than their husbands (M = .10) to report problems stemming from differential achievement [F(1,336) = 8.75, $p < .01$]. However, number of children was not related to the reported incidence of these problems, either separately or in interaction with other terms.

Wives were also less satisfied with their rate of professional advancement than were their husbands [F(1,345) = 5.05, $p < .05$; m = 1.83 and 1.59 for wives and husbands, respectively]. In addition, there was a marginally significant interaction between sex and number of children [F(3,345) = 2.45, $p < .10$]. Examination of the relevant means indicated a tendency for wives to feel less satisfied as number of children increased, while husbands' satisfaction with rate of advancement was unrelated to number of children (if anything, there was an opposite tendency for husbands).

Wives were less satisfied (M = 1.91) than their husbands (M = 1.42) with regard to their opportunity to interact with their colleagues [F(1,345) = 4.46, $p < .01$]. No other significant effects were observed for this variable.

Wives were also considerably less satisfied with their freedom to pursue long-range job goals [F(1,345) = 16.88, $p < .001$; M = 1.85 and 1.48 for wives and husbands, respectively]. In addition, satisfaction with the ability to pursue long-range job goals varied as a function of years since PhD [F(2,345) = 3.08, $p < .05$], with those finishing in the last nine years expressing greater dissatisfaction (M = 1.75)

FAMILY SIZE, SATISFACTION, AND PRODUCTIVITY IN DUAL-CAREER COUPLES

than those who had completed their training earlier (M = 1.56 and 1.57 for those in the 10–18 and 19+ years since final degree groups, respectively). Satisfaction was also related to number of children, with those having more children expressing greater dissatisfaction [$F(3,345)$ = 3.45, p <.05; M = 1.53, 1.62, 1.71, and 1.68, for those with 0, 1, 2, and 3+ children, respectively].

The single observed effect for the question concerning satisfaction with the regard of colleagues was a sex-by-years-since-final-degree interaction [$F(2,336)$ = 3.18, p < .05]; wives who were more recent graduates were more dissatisfied than their husbands, while among earlier graduates the husbands were more dissatisfied than the wives.

Satisfaction with the time available for professional activities was significantly related to sex [$F(1,336)$ = 10.89, p < .001], years since final degree [$F(2,336)$ = 3.46, p < .05], and number of children [$F(3,336)$ = 6.12, p < .001]. As with most of the job-related satisfaction measures, wives were more dissatisfied (M = 1.82) than husbands (M = 1.51). Those who had obtained their final degree more recently were less satisfied than those who had held their final degree for the longest period of time (M = 1.73, 1.74, and 1.46, for 0–9, 10–18, and 19+ years, respectively). And finally, those who had no children were more satisfied than those with children, although the total number of children seemed to make little difference (m = 1.39, 1.68, 1.84, and 1.72, for those with 0, 1, 2, and 3+ children, respectively).

Professional Productivity

Two measures of professional productivity were examined in this study: number of articles published and number of convention papers presented. Although these two measures are perhaps more relevant measures of productivity for psychologists in academic settings than for those who are professionally employed, they provide a common basis for evaluating productivity, and are not biased by the distribution of nonacademically employed psychologists across the various groups in our design.

Analyses of these two variables indicated that husbands both published more [$F(1,368)$ = 30.02, p < .001; m = 17.6 and 6.9 for husbands and wives, respectively] and presented more convention papers [$F(1,368)$ = 17.45, p < .001; M = 9.56 and 3.54, respectively]. Not surprisingly, productivity was related to years since final degree

[$F(2,368) = 27.13$ and $19.50, p < .001$ in both cases, for publications and papers, respectively]. There was also a tendency for the difference between husbands' and wives' number of publications to increase as a function of years since final degree, revealed in the interaction between these two terms [$F(2,368) = 4.11 \ p < .02$]. However, there was no effect of number of children on these measures of productivity, either alone or in interaction.

DISCUSSION

Differences between husbands and wives were obtained on nine of the 12 measures examined in this study: Wives expressed less satisfaction with the amount of time available for domestic activities, for avocational activities, and for professional activities; they reported greater problems caused by differential achievement; they were more dissatisfied with their rate of advancement, opportunity to interact with colleagues, freedom to pursue long-range job goals; and they had published fewer articles and presented fewer papers at conventions. Satisfaction with the regard of colleagues was also related to sex, but in interaction with years since final degree: Younger wives and older husbands expressed the greater dissatisfaction on this measure. However, these effects are not easily interpretable because of the large differences between husbands and wives in PhD completion rate and current employment status. Consequently, we will not concern ourselves with these effects in our discussion.

Of considerably greater interest to the present research are the effects of family size on measures of satisfaction and productivity, whether separately or in interaction. While such effects were obtained less consistently than sex differences, those items for which family-size effects were obtained refer quite consistently to the allocation of time—for domestic activities, for avocations, for family, and for professional activities. In all cases, those with more children report greater dissatisfaction with the amount of time available.

Family size was also related to measures of time allocation over longer periods. Satisfaction with one's rate of advancement can be considered, in part, to reflect prior allocation of time to job and to other requirements; those who are less satisfied may be considered to have had to allocate less time to job-related activities because of demands from other areas. On this item there was a directionally different effect of family size for husbands and wives: As family size increased, husbands' satisfaction with rate of advancement increased slightly, while wives' satisfaction decreased.

Satisfaction with the freedom to pursue long-range job goals was also related to family size. However, on this item there was no significant interaction between sex of respondent and family size; both husband and wife reported feeling less freedom as family size increased. In a sense, this item may be considered as a measure of the feeling that one has control over the allocation of one's time in the future: Those with children felt less free to make future plans without consideration of others.

The data indicate that family size is not related to productivity. Although husbands were consistently more productive than wives, number of children was not associated with number of articles or convention papers for either sex. A more detailed examination of possible differential effects of number of children on productivity was made by examining this relationship separately within each age group. However, there was still no evidence for an effect of number of children on productivity.

The relationships between family size and the various dependent variables may be considered as a problem of time allocation with limited resources. As the number of children increases, the time requirements to meet domestic demands also increase, with a concomitant decrease in the amount of time availabe for other activities. This shift in time demands can be met by both members of the dual-career couple sharing the extra requirements equally, or these extra requirements may be distributed unequally. The present data suggest that the latter solution is the more common: As the domestic demands increase, the burden for meeting these extra requirements falls disproportionately on the wife and is expressed in her increased dissatisfaction with both job and domestic activities.

The general absence of interactions of years since final degree with sex or number of children suggests that this inequality has not diminished to any noticeable extent over time, despite the increasing awareness of women's rights and the promotion of sexual equality in more recent years. Perhaps it is a sign of a general positive societal change that there were not more or larger interactions between sex and family size. However, it is surprising to find that even in couples where both husband and wife are professionally trained (and presumably in a field where they would be relatively more accepting of the concept of sexual equality), the evidence suggests that traditional sex roles still appear to be the basis for allocating responsibility for child care.

REFERENCES

Bryson, R., Bryson, J., Licht, M., & Licht, B. The professional pair: Husband and wife psychologists. *American Psychologist*, 1976, *31*, 10–16.
Hoffman, L., & Nye, F. W. *Working mothers*. San Francisco: Jossey-Boss, 1974.

A Study of Husbands and Wives from Dual-Career and Traditional-Career Families

Willa R. Huser and Claude W. Grant

University of Utah

Husbands and wives of dual-career families were compared with husbands and wives of traditional-career families on the variables of inner-directedness, self-actualizing values, existentiality, self-regard, and self-acceptance. Also, comparisons between the two sets of couples were made on shared and unshared interests. Our findings indicate that the husbands and wives in our sample of dual-career families do not differ in major ways from our sample of husbands and wives of traditional-career families; however, in every instance of difference, the direction of difference supports the view that husbands and wives of dual-career families are more inner-directed and flexible in applying personal values than husbands and wives of traditional-career families.

Since women first began in large numbers to hold jobs outside of the home and especially since the latest feminist awakenings there has been an increasing interest in dual-career families. Sociologists and psychologists are writing both scholarly and popular literature about women's working as related to happiness and unhappiness (Meredith, 1967; Peters, 1969), dynamics of achievement motivation in women (Fontana, 1970; Parker, 1971; Shelton, 1967), possible effects of working mothers on children (Clavan, 1972; Sweet, 1968), role perception and conflicts of working or nonworking women (Morgan, 1962; Profant, 1968; Zaro, 1971), personality traits of

Willa R. Huser and Claude W. Grant are affiliated with the University of Utah. Requests for reprints should be sent to Claude W. Grant, University of Utah, Salt Lake City, Utah 84112.

Psychology of Women Quarterly, Vol. 3(1) Fall 1978
0361-6843/78/1500-0078$00.95 © 1978 Human Sciences Press

women who work or who choose not to (Avila, 1964; Birnbaum, 1971; Glick, 1965; Hudson, 1963; Ohlbaum, 1971), childhood or background factors of women who work or who do not (Eyde, 1959; Ginn, 1968; Kriger, 1971; Schneider, 1962), the impact of working on the family structure and vice versa (Holmstrom, 1972; Whitehurst, 1963), and the origin of home or career commitment in women (Almquist, 1969; Paulsen, 1967; Tinsley, 1972).

There are a number of reasons for the greatly increased attention that these and related areas have been receiving. First and quite obviously, there are proportionately more women than ever before in the labor force of this country, and the record of the past years indicates a trend in female employment that will, in all probability, continue indefinitely into the future (Ray, 1972). More women want to work and are preparing themselves for careers in anticipation of such employment. Roby (1972) reports that 40.4% of all bachelor's or first professional degrees in higher education and 33.8% of all master's degrees go to women. A number of studies have established that a higher level of education among women leads to a higher level of commitment to work (Hubback, 1957; Myrdal & Klein, 1968).

It would appear that interest in careers for women is gaining increased respectability, especially during the past decade. There is increasing publicity given to the difficulties inherent in a woman's having as her sole interest and commitment her husband, children, and home, especially in her more mature years (Birnbaum, 1971). However, despite a great deal of talk and the numerous words that have been written about "women's rights" and "equal opportunity" in the United States, it is still difficult to have two careers in one family. For the most part, it is assumed (for middle- and upper-class families, at any rate) that only one spouse will be truly committed to a career, and that that one will be, virtually without exception, the husband (Holmstrom, 1972). The wife is assumed to have either no career at all or one that is placed in a position that is of pronouncedly less importance than her husband's career—if his professional advancement requires moving to another part of the country, they move; if the babysitter fails to show up when both spouses have business appointments, she cancels hers; if pressures begin to occur as a result of both spouses working, she quits (Holmstrom, 1972; Rapoport & Rapoport, 1971). Due to the unique and in many ways stressful isolation of the small, modern "nuclear family," child rearing, which was formerly shared by other significant people in and around the family as well, has now become the sole responsibility of the parents and specifically of the wife. This has reached an extreme

80

A STUDY OF DUAL-CAREER AND TRADITIONAL-CAREER FAMILIES

in the so-called "bedroom suburbs," where the wife almost single-handedly raises the children while the husband spends hours commuting daily to and from work or even stays in a rented apartment during the week.

Furthermore, rigidities in the structure of the academic and professional world make two careers very difficult to achieve (Holmstrom, 1972). Single-minded devotion to a career is expected with advancement as the reward, and subordination of other interests is taken for granted.

With the societal expectation that the wife raise the children, keep the home clean and comfortable, and feed the family, it is obviously difficult for a women to be single-minded about a career. This dilemma is intensified by the lack of child-care centers, the isolation of the nuclear family, unwillingness on the part of employers to hire less than full-time personnel, the tendency of universities to favor full-time students in professional training, etc. Indeed, many professional positions require that the husband have a wife whose time and energy are devoted to the job as well, as for example with political figures, high executives in companies, and presidents of universities. She is expected to look and act the part of wife and mother in a way that is enhancing to him, to entertain and be entertained by others who are professionally important, and to be committed to helping her husband in every possible way to advance in his chosen field. Obviously, since no system has yet been devised for the career-committed woman to have a wife, she is severely limited if her ambitions include one of the many careers and professions where a wife is necessary.

Because the increased interest in dual-career families is by necessity focused upon women and their home/career options, considerable research and writing in the area is centered upon women particularly. (Dual-career is defined as those families in which both husband and wife are pursuing full-time, paid professions.) Various crucial aspects of the career-oriented woman have been examined: Ginn (1968) studied the effects of identification and/or family attitudes on the vocational development of women; Fontana (1970) looked at achievement motivation and women; Parker (1971) studied the concept of "fear of success" in women; Almquist and Angrist (1970) looked at women who choose male-dominated occupations; the differences between married professional women and housewives were examined by Shelton (1967); Arnott (1972) looked at married women's choices for full-time homemaking or "dual roles" in terms of exchange theory; Harder (1969) examined self-actualization among married women; Kriger (1971) attempted to discover the relationship between perceptions of child-rearing attitudes and achievement needs as they influence a woman's decision to become a homemaker or a career woman; family-oriented and career women were studied by Birnbaum (1971), and Tinsley (1972) looked at differences between women who are home oriented and women who are career oriented.

Few studies focus on both the husband and the wife and their interaction in dual-career families. Noteworthy are studies by Holstrom (1970) and Rapoport and Rapoport (1971). Problems and strains growing out of interaction within the dual-career family were explored in each of these two studies. The authors find, among other things, that dual-career marriages experience zones of stress growing out of housekeeping tasks, child-care, leisure activities, modification of career involvement, norms and expectations of society, dilemmas of identity, social dilemmas, role-conflict dilemmas, and lack of leisure time. Holmstrom (1970) states: "It is frequently alleged that all opportunities are open to women—even married women—and that they just have not taken advantage of time. However . . . it is not surprising that there are so few two-career families; the surprising things is that any such families exist at all" (p. 5).

In view of the structural and attitudinal difficulties that members of the dual-career family face, we may ask: why do some couples choose this deviant lifestyle? What psychological traits do they possess that are different from those of other couples? In what ways are their attitudes and self-perceptions at variance with the more usual (traditional) couple?

STATEMENT OF PROBLEM

The major purpose of this study was to determine whether or not husbands and wives of dual-career families differed from husbands and wives of traditional families on some selected characteristics, as measured by the Personal Orientation Inventory (Shostrom, 1966), specifically: (1) inner-directedness, or the tendency for a person to act upon and be guided by his or her own principles and motives in contrast to responding to external pressures; (2) self-actualizing values, or the extent to which an individual holds and lives by values of self-actualizing people; (3) existentiality, or one's ability to situationally or existentially react without rigid adherence to principles, i.e., flexibility in applying personal values; (4) self-regard, or the affirmation of the self due to worth or strength; and (5) self-acceptance, or acceptance of oneself despite weaknesses and deficiencies. Other purposes were to determine if there are differences between the two sets of husbands and wives in terms of the interests and leisure-time activities that couples share or participate in on an individual basis, and to determine the similarity of their responses to a set of forced-choice items reflecting personal orientation vs. other orientation.

METHOD

Sample

The sample consisted of a total of 83 couples; 43 couples were in the traditional-family category and 40 couples were in the dual-career family category. Subjects were obtained by contacting, by letter, 1,344 faculty members of the University of Utah. The letter stated the purpose of the study and requested participation by the faculty member and his/her spouse.

Four hundred and thirty-nine faculty members responded, expressing a willingness to participate. From information requested in the initial letter, the investigators selected the 100 couples, 50 defined as dual-career marriages and 50 defined as traditional marriages, that most suited the purposes of the study. Respondents not selected for the study were sent a post card thanking them for their willingness to participate.

Those couples who were chosen to be participants were sent an envelope with a copy of the Personal Orientation Inventory test booklet, two answer sheets clearly marked for each individual, a short questionnaire, a cover letter of instructions, and a stamped return envelope. One week later a follow-up letter was mailed to each couple directing their attention to completion of the information, and a week after that all couples who had not yet sent in their information were contacted personally by telephone. A total of 83 couples did complete the inventory and the questionnaire; 43 couples were in the traditional category and 40 in the dual-career category. This information provided the data on which the study was based.

The ages of respondents in the sample ranged from 35 to 55. This range was selected to give time for participants to have become professionally established. Also, by the age of 35 there is a greater likelihood that personality traits and attitudes will be constant and lifelong.

The participants of the two samples were similar in that they all lived in the immediate vicinity of Salt Lake City, they all had at least a bachelor's degree, they were between the ages of 35 and 55, and at least one member of each husband-wife combination held a faculty position at the University of Utah. The two groups were dissimilar in that while the wives from the dual-career families held professional positions, the wives from the traditional families were not working nor were they anticipating working. They described themselves as housewives or homemakers. Information about past work history was not obtained. Another difference involved educational level; while all wives had a minimum of a bachelor's degree, 33 of the 40 dual-career wives held a master's or higher degree, but only eight of the 43 traditional-career wives had degrees beyond the bachelor's degree. Among the husbands, 41 of the 43 in the traditional-career category held degrees beyond the master's degree in comparison with 25 of the 40 in the dual-career category.

The occupations of traditional-career husbands and dual-career husbands and wives are shown in Table 1. The occupations of all husbands and all but four working wives are classified as professional. The nonprofessional positions are secretary (1), travel agent (1), and technician (2).

Instruments

The Personal Orientation Inventory (POI) was the primary instrument used in this study. This instrument was developed specifically to fill the need

TABLE 1

Careers

| Career | Husbands | | Career | Wives |
	Traditional	Dual-Career		Dual-Career
University Professor	38	19	Univ. Prof.	14
Physicians (Prof.)	4	0	Social Worker	2
Psychiatrist (Prof.)	1	0	Physician	1
Psychologist	0	3	Admin. Secretary	1
Ecologist	0	1	Counselor/Psych.	4
Accountant	0	1	Architect/Artist	1
Businessman	0	4	Travel Agent	1
Management	0	4	Program Director	1
Educator	0	6	Technician	2
Engineer	0	2	Educator	12
			Writer	1
	43	40		40

The 43 Traditional wives listed their occupations as housewives, homemakers, unemployed.

A STUDY OF DUAL-CAREER AND TRADITIONAL-CAREER FAMILIES

for a comprehensive measure of values and attitudes as they reflect the development of self-actualization (Shostrom, 1966). The inventory consists of 150 forced-choice (two-choice) items that focus upon value and behavior judgments of the individual.

The specific traits assessed by the POI that are of interest to the investigators in this study are: inner-directedness, self-actualizing values, existentiality, self-regard, and self-acceptance. Other information obtained from the subjects were leisure time and social activities shared with spouse interests not shared with spouse, and the percent of agreement between spouses in answers to the items of the POI.

RESULTS

Husbands in the dual-career families were compared with husbands in traditional families, and wives in dual-career families were compared with wives in traditional families on the selected scales of the POI. Comparisons were also made on shared and unshared interests; item analyses of the 150 items of the POI were run comparing husbands from the two categories and wives from the two categories, and the percent of agreement for the direction of response to the items was determined for each set of husbands and wives.

TABLE 2

Comparisons of POI Scores for Husbands

		Traditional	Dual-Career	t-value
Other-Directedness	Mean	88.6	93.9	1.96*
	S.D.	10.4	14.2	
Self-Actualizing Values	Mean	21.2	21.3	0.11
	S.D.	2.5	3.4	
Existentiality	Mean	20.6	22.8	2.18*
	S.D.	3.8	5.4	
Self-Regard	Mean	12.9	13.6	1.19
	S.D.	2.6	2.6	
Self-Acceptance	Mean	16.2	18.3	2.77**
	S.D.	3.5	3.2	

*P .05
**P .01

WILLA R. HUSER, CLAUDE W. GRANT

Comparisons of POI scores for husbands are presented in Table 2. Husbands from dual-career families were found to differ significantly from husbands from traditional families on the POI scales of inner-directedness, existentiality, and self-acceptance. In all cases dual-career husbands scored higher than traditional. There were no differences on the scales of self-actualizing values or self-regard.

Wives from dual-career families were found to differ significantly from wives from traditional families on the POI scale of inner-directedness (dual-career scoring higher than traditional). There were no differences on the scales of self-actualizing values, existentiality, self-regard, and self-acceptance. Scores are presented in Table 3.

No significant differences were found between husbands and wives of dual-career families vs. husbands and wives of traditional families in terms of the number of interests they listed as shared or the number of interests listed as unshared, nor were there significant differences in the types of interests, either shared or unshared (individual, social, physical).

The item analysis comparing husbands with husbands and wives with wives yielded the following: There were only eight items of the 150 on which the two sets of husbands differed significantly, $p < .05$. One would expect this number by chance. On the other hand, it is significant that on each of these eight items the dual-career husbands

TABLE 3

Comparisons of POI Scores for Wives

		Traditional	Dual-Career	t-value
Inner-Directedness	Mean	86.5	92.8	2.19*
	S.D.	11.6	14.8	
Self-Actualizing Values	Mean	20.1	21.2	1.54
	S.D.	2.8	3.8	
Existentiality	Mean	20.1	22.1	1.80
	S.D.	4.5	5.8	
Self-Regard	Mean	12.8	13.3	0.74
	S.D.	4.5	5.8	
Self-Acceptance	Mean	12.8	13.3	0.74
	S.D.	2.4	3.3	

*P .05

A STUDY OF DUAL-CAREER AND TRADITIONAL-CAREER FAMILIES

responded more frequently in the self-actualized direction. The two sets of wives differed significantly ($p < .05$) on 20 of the items. This is a larger number than one would expect by chance, and on 18 of the 20 items the dual-career wives responded more frequently in the self-actualized direction.

There was greater agreement on the direction of responses to the POI items between husbands and wives of dual-career families than between husbands and wives of traditional families (73.1% agreement vs. 70.7%, $z = 2.96$, $p < .01$).

DISCUSSION

The husbands and wives in our sample of dual-career families, while similar in many ways to the husbands and wives in our sample of traditional families, do differ in some important ways. In every instance of difference, the direction of difference supports the view that husbands and wives of dual-career families are more inner-directed and flexible in applying personal values than husbands and wives of traditional families.

The POI scales on which the two sets of husbands differ are inner-directedness, existentiality, and self-acceptance. The one scale of the five used in this study on which the two sets of wives differ is inner-directedness. The items identified through item analysis on which the two sets of husbands and two sets of wives differ are items characteristic of inner-directedness, flexibility in applying personal values, and existentiality.

In general, the two groups shared a number of important characteristics of the self-actualized person. Scores on the POI scales demonstrate this, as do the level of education and the occupations of group members. The one differentiating factor between the two groups is the fact that the wives in the traditional families were not working; they viewed themselves as homemakers. Despite the other marked similarities between the two groups, obtained differences on some of the POI scales as well as differences in responding to specific items of the POI indicate predictable differences in attitude and self-concept between them; also, husband and wife agreement in direction of responses to individual items of the POI suggests a closer identity between dual-career couples than traditional couples.

There are many factors related to the participants in this study that would seem to reduce the likelihood of finding consistent differences of the kind reported in this study: (1) all participants live in a rather conservative community, (2) all husbands hold professional positions, (3) at least one person in each husband-wife pair is employed at the University of Utah, (4) all participants hold a bachelor's degree or higher, and (5) they are all between the ages of 35 and 55. Despite these mitigating factors, personality characteristics that allow two career-oriented people to marry and continue their careers are in some respects measurably different from personality characteristics of couples where one, the wife, is not a career person.

From reviewing the literature related to this study, the reader could expect to find the differences that we have found here. Although as a people we supposedly support the concept of the career woman and dual-career families, there is nevertheless a powerful and pervasive pressure for individuals to conform to societal roles in which the wife is a mother, at home, and subservient to the husband and the husband is the bread winner and the dominant person in the family. Those individuals who have been able to resist internalizing some of the larger society's values and through personal choice join in dual-career marriages can be expected to be more inner-directed and flexible in applying personal values than those individuals whose marriages fit the "traditional" model. On the other hand, because the traditional wife obtains considerable personal satisfaction and public exposure through the profession of her husband, it should be expected that wives of traditional marriages in which the husbands hold recognized professional positions at a major university should experience considerable self-acceptance and personal esteem through his position. We believe this to be the case for our sample of traditional wives in this study. On the POI scales, the scores for the traditional wives are more similar to those for the dual-career wives than are the scores for the traditional husbands and the dual-career husbands. It would seem that for a man to choose a career-oriented woman for a wife marks him as being quite different, in a self-actualized direction, from other men as a group. It would also seem, from examining responses to individual items of the POI, that there are major differences between dual-career wives and traditional wives related to self-actualization.

REFERENCES

Almquist, E. M. Occupational choice and career salience among college women. (Doctoral dissertation, University of Kansas, 1969). *Dissertation Abstracts International,* 1969, *30* 06-A, 2634. (University Microfilms No. 69-21484)

A STUDY OF DUAL-CAREER AND TRADITIONAL-CAREER FAMILIES

Almquist, E. M., & Angrist, S. S. Career salience and atypicality of occupational choice among college women. *Journal of Marriage and Family*, 1970, *32*, 242–249.

Arnott, C. C. Married women and the pursuit of profit: An exchange theory perspective. *Journal of Marriage and the Family*, 1972, *34*, 122–130.

Avila, D. L. An inverted factor analysis of personality differences between career and homemaking oriented women. (Doctoral dissertation, The University of Nebraska Teachers College, 1964). *Dissertation Abstracts*, 1964, *25/01*, 609. (University Microfilms No. 64-08054)

Birnbaum, J. L. A. Life patterns, personality style, and self-esteem in gifted family oriented and career committed women. (Doctoral dissertation, The University of Michigan, 1971). *Dissertation Abstracts International*, 1971, *32/03-B*, 1834. (University Microfilms No. 71-23698)

Clavan, S. Impact of feminism on American family structure. (Doctoral dissertation, Temple University, 1972). *Dissertation Abstracts International*, 1972, *32/12-A*, 7106. (University Microfilms No. 72-17684)

Eyde, L. Work values and background factors as predictors of women's desire to work. (Doctoral dissertation, Ohio State University, 1959). *Dissertation Abstracts*, 1959, *20/09*, 3829. (University Microfilms No. 60-00736)

Fontana, G. L. J. An investigation into the dynamics of achievement motivation in women. (Doctoral dissertation, The University of Michigan, 1970). *Dissertation Abstracts International*, 1970, *32/03-B*, 1821. (University Microfilms No. 71-23754)

Ginn, F. W. Career motivation and role perception of women as related to parental role expectation and parental status discrepancy. (Doctoral dissertation. The Catholic University of America, 1968). *Dissertation Abstracts*, 1968, *29/12-B*, 4845. (University Microfilms No. 69-09159)

Glick, R. Practitioners and non-practitioners in a group of women physicians. (Doctoral dissertation, Western Reserve University, 1965). *Dissertation Abstracts*, 1965, *26/11*, 6845. (University Microfilms No. 66-03031)

Harder, J. M. Self-actualization, mood, and personality adjustment in married women. (Doctoral dissertation, Columbia University, 1969). *Dissertation Abstracts International*, 1969, *31/02-B*, 897. (University Microfilms (No. 70-13771)

Holmstrom, L. L. *Intertwining career patterns of husbands and wives in certain professions.* Unpublished doctoral dissertation, Brandeis University, 1970.

Holmstrom, L. L. *The two-career family.* Cambridge, Mass: Schenkman Publishing Co., 1972.

Hubback, J. *Wives who went to college.* London: Heinemann Publishers, 1957.

Hudson, J. B. Feminine roles and family norms in a small city. (Doctoral dissertation, Cornell University, 1963). *Dissertation Abstracts*, 1963, *24/05*, 2180. (University Microfilms No. 63-08107)

Kriger, S. F. Need achievement and perceived parental child rearing attitudes of career women and homemakers. (Doctoral dissertation, Ohio State University, 1971). *Dissertation Abstracts International*, 1971, *32/11-B*, 6621. (University Microfilms No. 72-15235)

Meredith, A. C. Comparative lifestyles of women: Secretarial career versus career and marriage. (Doctoral dissertation, The University of Southern California, 1967). *Dissertation Abstracts*, 1967, *28/07-B*, 3063. (University Microfilms No. 67-17686)

Morgan, D. D. Perception of role conflicts and self concepts among career and noncareer college educated women. (Doctoral dissertation, Columbia University, 1962). *Dissertation Abstracts*, 1962, *23/05*, 1816. (University Microfilms No. 62-04242)

Myrdal, A., & Klein, V. *Women's two roles.* London: Routledge and Kegan Paul Ltd., 1968.

Ohlbaum, J. S. Self-concepts, value characteristics, and self-actualization of professional and non-professional women. (Doctoral dissertation, United States International University, 1971). *Dissertation Abstracts International*, 1971, *32/02-B*, 1221. (University Microfilms No. 71-14181)

Parker, V. J. Fear of success, sex-role orientation of the task, and competition condition as variables affecting women's performance in achievement-oriented situations. (Doctoral dissertation, Ohio University, 1971). *Dissertation Abstracts International*, 1971, *32/09-B*, 5495. (University Microfilms No. 72-09593)

WILLA R. HUSER, CLAUDE W. GRANT

Paulsen, D. L. The career commitment of twelfth grade girls. (Doctoral dissertation, Yale University, 1967). *Dissertation Abstracts*, 1967, *28/10-A*, 4290. (University Microfilms No. 68-05200)

Peters, J. R. Constituents of experience in job happiness and unhappiness in employed women. (Doctoral dissertation, Duquesne University, 1969). *Dissertation Abstracts International*, 1969, *31/03-B*, 1580. (University Microfilms No. 70-16899)

Profant, P. M. Sex differences and sex role stereotypes as related to professional career goals. (Doctoral dissertation, Ohio State University, 1968). *Dissertation Abstracts International*, 1968, *30/01-B*, 388. (University Microfilms No. 69-11695)

Rapoport, R., & Rapoport, R. *Dual-career families*. Baltimore, Md: Penguin Books, 1971.

Ray, L. The American woman in mass media: How much emancipation and what does it mean? in *Toward a sociology of women*. Safilios-Rothschild, C., ed. Lexington, Mass.: Xerox College Publishing Company, 1972.

Roby, P. Structural and internalized barriers to women in higher education. *Toward a sociology of women*. Lexington, Mass.: Xerox College Publishing Company, 1972.

Schneider, L. R. The relationship between identification with mother and home or career orientation in women. (Doctoral dissertation, Columbia University, 1962). *Dissertation Abstracts*, 1962, *23/05*, 1787. (University Microfilms No. 62-04247)

Shelton, P. B. Achievement motivation in professional women. (Doctoral dissertation, University of California, 1967). *Dissertation Abstracts*, 1967, *28/10-A*, 4274. (University Microfilms No. 68-05821)

Shostrom, E. *Personal Orientation Inventory*. San Diego, Calif.: Educational and Industrial Testing Service, 1966.

Sweet, J. A. Family composition and the labor force activity of married women in the United States. (Doctoral dissertation, The University of Michigan, 1968). *Dissertation Abstracts International*, 1968, *30/02-A*, 837. (University Microfilms No. 69-12250)

Tinsley, D. E. Characteristics of women with different patterns of career orientation. (Doctoral dissertation, University of Minnesota, 1972). *Dissertation Abstracts International*, 1972, *33/06-B*, 2797. (University Microfilms No. 72-32322)

Whitehurst, R. N. Employed mother's influences on working class family structure. (Doctoral dissertation, Purdue University, 1963). *Dissertation Abstracts*, 1963, *24/12*, 5600. (University Microfilms No. 64-05774)

Zaro, J. S. An experimental study of role conflict in women. (Doctoral dissertation, the University of Connecticut, 1971). *Dissertation Abstracts International*, 1971, *33/06-B*, 2828. (University Microfilms no. 72-32173)

Wives' Employment Status and Marital Adjustment: Yet Another Look

Graham L. Staines

The University of Michigan

Joseph H. Pleck

University of Massachusetts at Amherst

Linda J. Shepard and Pamela O'Connor

The University of Michigan

The effects of wives' employment status on wives' and husbands' evaluations of their own marital adjustment are examined in two recent national surveys. Working wives whose husbands also work report having wished they had married someone else and having thought of divorce significantly more often than housewives, but do not score significantly lower on ratings of marital satisfaction or marital happiness, or on four other specific components of marital adjustment. Wives' employment status does not significantly affect husbands' reports of marital adjustment. The negative effects of wives' employment on wives' reports of marital adjustment are then found to be restricted specifically to mothers of preschool children, and to wives with less than a high school diploma. No empirical support emerges for two major hypotheses to account for the negative effects of wives' employment on wives' marital adjustment in these two subgroups, one hypothesis concerning wives' role load and the second concerning wives' and husbands' attitudes toward wives' employment. There is some evidence, however, that these factors are moderators of the negative effects of wives' employment on

---

This research was supported in part by Grant No. 91-26-75-28 from the Employment and Training Administration, U.S. Department of Labor. We would like to thank the editors of this journal issue and the following colleagues for their helpful criticisms of an earlier draft of the manuscript: Angus Campbell, Elizabeth Douvan, Jane Hood, Richard Kulka, and Joseph Veroff. In addition, we wish to acknowledge the generous assistance of Laura Klem in planning the statistical analyses. The order of authorship for the first two authors was determined randomly. Requests for reprints should be sent to Graham L. Staines, Assistant Research Scientist, Survey Research Center, Institute for Social Research, Ann Arbor, Michigan 48106.

Psychology of Women Quarterly, Vol. 3(1) Fall 1978
0361-6843/78/1500-0090$00.9 © 1978 Human Sciences Press

wives' marital adjustment, in particular, that high role load moderates the negative effects of employment among mothers of preschool children.

Recent interest in families in which husband and wife both work for pay (i.e., dual-worker families) has revived the debate over whether a wife's work status affects her own or her husband's marital adjustment. To resolve this debate, studies must compare either working wives whose husbands also work (dual wives) with housewives whose husbands work (housewives), or working husbands of working wives (dual husbands) with working husbands of housewives (sole breadwinning husbands). Relevant studies must also contain psychological measures of marital adjustment and must analyze separately the marital adjustment reported by each spouse.

Thirteen previous studies have included zero-order comparisons on marital adjustment between the two groups of wives or the two groups of husbands. (This summary of the literature omits a number of studies that compared the marital adjustment of dual wives and housewives among mothers only, e.g., Feld, 1963, and Nye, 1959.) In some of the 13, a limited percentage of working wives whose husbands were not currently working were included along with the dual wives. All of the studies employed national or community-wide samples, drawn either through probability-sampling techniques or through cruder procedures that appear to have produced nearly representative samples. Whereas most of the 13 studies involved American samples, several were conducted in European settings. Regrettably, these 13 studies typically used quite different measures of marital adjustment. Such methodological variations notwithstanding, their findings are directionally consistent. Seven studies registered somewhat higher marital adjustment among housewives than dual wives (Buric & Zecevic, 1967; Campbell, Converse & Rodgers, 1976; Gover, 1963; Michel, 1967; Radloff, 1975; Safilios-Rothschild, 1967; Scanzoni, 1970), although only one of them (Gover, 1963) established the difference as significant. Four studies (Blood & Wolfe, 1960; Gross & Arvey, 1977; Haavio-Mannila, 1971; Orden & Bradburn, 1969) obtained trivial differences; another (Safilios-Rothschild, 1970) recorded only that there was no significant difference, and no study reported a significant reversal of the dominant pattern. Two studies of the marital adjustment of husbands (Axelson, 1963; Scanzoni, 1970) assigned an edge to sole breadwinners over dual husbands, significantly so in the earlier study, but a third study (Campbell et al., 1976) found no difference.

While zero-order comparisons among the marital groups hold

considerable interest, they may obscure more potent differences within specific subsamples. Twelve studies have examined the impact of wives' employment status on marital adjustment within one or more levels of education. Eleven of the 12 included comparisons among highly educated wives (i.e., largely college educated). They tend to indicate that the zero-order pattern noted above (better marital adjustment among housewives than dual wives) existed before 1960 among educated women (Chesser, 1956; Davis, 1929; Locke & Mackeprang, 1949 [study two]). Yet by around 1970, the studies of educated women suggested no clear advantage to housewives in that roughly as many studies found higher adjustment among dual wives (Burke & Weir, 1976; Campbell et al., 1976; Scanzoni, 1970) as found an advantage for housewives (Fogarty, Rapoport, & Rapoport, 1971; Tavris, 1971) or no advantage for either group (Tavris & Jayaratne, 1976; Feldman, 1965; Fidell, 1977a, 1977b). Even the three studies reporting significant differences for educated wives (Burke & Weir, 1976; Campbell et al., 1976; Fogarty et al., 1971) were inconsistent as to direction. Two studies reported on less educated wives, mainly wives without high school diplomas (Scanzoni, 1970; Hauenstein, 1976). Both studies were recent, and both pointed to an advantage in adjustment among housewives. Taken together, the recent studies concerning levels of education suggest that the decrement in marital adjustment of dual wives relative to housewives is greater among less educated than among better educated wives. As for husbands, the data on marital adjustment and education have conformed to no clear trend (Burke & Weir, 1976; Locke & Mackeprang, 1949 [study two]; Scanzoni, 1970).

Aside from education, unfortunately, the literature on wives' employment status and marital adjustment includes no systematic, cross-sectional evidence on other important control variables such as family life-cycle stage.

The present study makes within-sex comparisons of the marital adjustment of the four major married groups, using data from two recent, nationally representative surveys. The analysis first compares the marital adjustment of the two groups of wives and the two groups of husbands in each total sample (zero-order comparisons) and within each level of two control variables, family life cycle and education (first-order comparisons). The latter first-order analyses are designed to locate demographic subgroups in which zero-order differences among the married groups are heightened or reduced. Two general interpretations of significant differences in marital adjustment at the first-order level are investigated: (1) that wives' employment affects wives' marital adjustment by creating role overload among employed wives through the combined demands of their paid work and family roles, and (2) that wives' employment is associated with differences in marital adjustment because of wives' and husbands' attitudes concerning wives' current work and family roles. The general analytic strategy used here is Lazarsfeld's "elaboration model" (Babbie, 1973).

METHOD

Sample

The first dataset comes from the 1971 Quality of Life Survey conducted by the Survey Research Center, Ann Arbor, Michigan (Campbell et al., 1976). The survey involved interviews with a national probability sample of 2,164 persons, 18 years of age or older, living in households in the coterminous United States. For this first dataset, the four married groups were defined analytically as follows:

Dual wives. Wives currently married and employed whose husbands are currently employed (N=259).

Housewives. Wives currently married but not employed who classify themselves as housewives and whose husbands are currently employed (N=368).

Dual husbands. Husbands currently married and employed 20 or more hours per week whose wives are currently employed (N=203).

Sole breadwinning husbands. Husbands currently married and employed 20 or more hours per week whose wives are not currently employed (N=303).

The second dataset was likewise collected by the Survey Research Center and is a product of the 1973 Fall Omnibus Survey. This later survey used the same sampling and interviewing techniques and generated a national probability sample of 1,440 respondents. It distinguished only three married groups as follows:

Dual wives. Wives currently married and employed whose husbands are heads of household and are currently employed (N=195).

Housewives. Wives currently married but not employed whose husbands are heads of household and currently employed (N=234).

Sole breadwinning husbands and dual husbands (combined). Husbands currently married and employed 20 or more hours per week who are also heads of household (*N*=354).

Measures

Dependent Variables. The 1971 Quality of Life Survey contained seven of the eight dependent measures analyzed in this paper. As regards global measures of marital adjustment, respondents were asked how satisfied they were with their marriages (*marital satisfaction*), whether they had ever wished they had married someone else (*wish married another*), and whether the thought of getting a divorce had ever crossed their minds (*think of divorce*). As to specific components of marital adjustment, respondents indicated how frequently they disagreed with their spouses about money (*financial disagreements*), whether they thought their spouses understood them well (*understood by spouse*), whether they thought they understood their spouses well (*understand spouse*), and how much companionship they had with their spouses (*companionship*). Full details on these dependent variables in the Quality of Life Survey, and on the control variables from the same survey to be described shortly, appear in Campbell et al. (1976).

The 1973 Omnibus Survey included only one global measure of marital adjustment, *marital happiness*. Respondents were asked: "Taking everything together, how happy would you say your marriage is?" (Possible answers were: not too happy, happy, very happy, extremely happy.)

First-order Control Variables. Two variables were employed in both datasets as first-order controls. The first, *family life cycle,* contained four categories: under 30 and no children, parent of a preschool child (aged six or under), parent of a school-age (aged seven–18) but not a preschool child, and 30 and over with no children living at home. The second, level of *education,* likewise had four categories: less than a high school diploma, high school diploma, some college education but no degree, and college degree or above. degree or above.

Second-order Control Variables. Wives' role load. The 1971 Quality of Life Survey provided one item interpretable as a measure of role load among wives. It asked wives how often they felt rushed even to do the things they had to do (*feel rushed*).

For mothers only, the 1973 Omnibus Survey included two items generating the following measure of the role load of wives: *want more help from husbands,* scored as high load when wives wished their husbands would do either more child care ("give you more help taking care of your children") or more housework ("give you more help with the daily household chores"). Other analyses of these two items are available in Robinson, Yerby, Feiweger, and Somerick (in press).

Attitudes to wives' present roles. Another set of second-order control variables pertain to attitudes toward wives' present roles. The Quality of Life Survey incorporated two questions that jointly measured *wives' role commitment*. Interviewers asked dual wives whether or not they would continue to work if they had enough money to live comfortably for the rest of their lives. They inquired of housewives whether they would take paid employment if they could have someone take care of things at home. Dual wives who chose to continue working and housewives who elected to stay home were both scored high on role commitment. This survey also included a pair of parallel but not entirely comparable items tapping *wives' role satisfaction*. Dual wives' role satisfaction was inferred from their reported level of satisfaction with their jobs. For housewives, role satisfaction was assessed by an item on satisfaction with their homemaking and housework, using an identical response scale.

The Omnibus Survey contained a measure of *husbands' attitudes to their wives' present roles*. All wives were asked: "How does your husband feel about your working at a job at least half-time? Is he very much in favor of it, somewhat in favor of it, neither in favor of nor against it, somewhat against it, or very much against it?" Dual wives working at least half-time were scored as having a husband who approved of their current role for the first two response categories, a husband who was neutral for the third category, and a husband who disapproved for the fourth and fifth categories. Conversely, housewives were considered to have a husband who approved of their current role for the last two categories, a husband who was neutral for the third category, and a husband who disapproved for the first two categories.

RESULTS AND DISCUSSION

Zero-order Differences in Marital Adjustment

Table 1 compares the two groups of wives and the two groups of husbands on various measures of marital adjustment. In the analyses reported here, all dual wives are grouped together. A preliminary analysis compared the marital adjustment of dual wives employed 35 or more hours per week (approximately 70% of all dual wives in the two surveys), dual wives employed 20–34 hours per week (18%), and dual wives employed 1–19 hours per week (12%). Although limited by the small sample sizes in the two part-time subgroups, these analyses found no significant differences among the three subgroups of dual wives on any of the measures of marital adjustment. Table 1 shows that dual wives do not differ significantly from housewives on the two global measures of adjustment that evaluate marriage as a

Table 1

Mean Scores on Global and Specific Measures of Marital Adjustment for Wives and Husbands, by Wives' Employment Status[a]

Global Measures	Dual Wives	House-wives	Difference (DW-HW)	t	Dual Husbands	Sole Bread-winners	Difference (DH-SB)	t
			Quality of Life Survey 1971					
Marital satisfaction	6.06 (259)	6.23 (364)	-.17	-1.76	6.30 (201)	6.36 (303)	-.06	-.68
Wish married another	4.31 (259)	4.58 (364)	-.27	-3.65**	4.55 (201)	4.54 (302)	.01	.12
Think of divorce	4.30 (259)	4.48 (364)	-.18	-2.51*	4.56 (201)	4.55 (302)	.01	.21
			Omnibus Survey 1973					
Marital happiness	2.86 (194)	2.91 (232)	-.05	-.66	2.93[b] (351)			

Table 1--(continued)

Specific Measures	Dual Wives	House-wives	Difference (DW-HW)	t	Dual Husbands	Sole Bread-winners	Difference (DH-SB)	t
				Quality of Life Survey 1971				
Financial disagreements	3.65 (259)	3.60 (368)	.05	.66	3.64 (203)	3.65 (303)	-.01	-.05
Understood by spouse	3.29 (259)	3.26 (366)	.03	.41	3.40 (203)	3.41 (303)	-.01	-.09
Understand spouse	3.36 (259)	3.42 (367)	-.06	-.98	3.34 (202)	3.33 (303)	.01	.25
Companionship	3.84 (258)	3.87 (367)	-.03	-.30	3.81 (203)	3.75 (301)	.06	.61

Note: In this and all subsequent tables, scoring has been reversed on items where necessary so that high score means good adjustment.

[a]In this and all subsequent tables, minor variations across variables in the sample size of any one group or subgroup may be attributed to missing data cases.

[b]In the Omnibus Survey, dual husbands and sole breadwinner husbands could not be distinguished.

*p < .05.

WIVES' EMPLOYMENT STATUS AND MARITAL ADJUSTMENT: YET ANOTHER LOOK

whole (*marital satisfaction* and *marital happiness*). Dual wives do, however, exhibit significantly poorer adjustment than housewives on both of the global measures that concern marital choices (*wish married another* and *think of divorce*). Yet no significant differences emerge between dual wives and housewives on any of the four specific measures of marital adjustment concerning disagreements about money, being understood by one's spouse, understanding one's spouse, and companionship with one's spouse.

The present results on wives' employment status and marital adjustment in the Quality of Life Survey differ from those reported by Campbell et al. (1976). In comparing employed wives and housewives, Campbell et al. concluded, "So far as our data can carry us, we find little reason to believe that on the average employment outside the home either enhances or diminishes a marriage, at least as the wives see it" (p. 425).

Campbell et al. contrasted employed wives and housewives by comparing the percentages in each group with responses indicating positive adjustment on the seven dependent measures available in their survey. On the two dependent measures revealing a significant mean difference between dual wives and housewives in the present analysis, Campbell et al. (1976) noted that 63% of employed wives and 74% of housewives said that they had never wished they had married someone else, and that 59% of employed wives and 68% of housewives indicated that the thought of divorce had never crossed their minds. Campbell et al. (1976) did not report significance tests for these differences and chose to deemphasize them in their interpretation. In addition to using a different summary statistic for comparing the two groups (percentages instead of means), Campbell et al.'s (1976) analysis also differed from the present one in that it included those wives whose husbands were not currently employed. As a result, sample sizes for Campbell et al.'s (1976) analysis (p. 423) were somewhat larger than those in the present analysis (445 vs. 368 housewives and 291 employed wives vs. 259 dual wives). These differences in group definition and statistical procedure both contribute to the discrepancies between the results from the two analyses.

As for husbands, Table 1 reveals that the employment of their wives is not significantly related to their level of marital adjustment on any of the seven dependent measures available in the Quality of Life Survey.

First-order Differences in Marital Adjustment

Tables 2 and 3 compare dual wives and housewives on the four global measures of marital adjustment within levels of two first-order

GRAHAM L. STAINES, *ET AL.*

Table 2

Mean Scores on Global Measures of Marital Adjustment for Wives,
by Wives' Employment Status and Family Life Cycle Stage

Family Life Cycle Stage	Dual Wives	House- wives	Difference (DW-HW)	t
Marital satisfaction (Quality of Life)				
Under 30 without children	6.37 (32)	6.27 (11)	.10	.34
Preschool children	5.83 (53)	6.18 (156)	-.35	-1.74
School age children	5.99 (101)	6.18 (107)	-.19	-1.09
30+ without children	6.18 (71)	6.37 (86)	-.19	-1.00
Wish married another (Quality of Life)				
Under 30 without children	4.47 (32)	4.46 (11)	.01	.04
Preschool children	3.87 (53)	4.48 (156)	-.61	-4.10**
School age children	4.35 (101)	4.63 (107)	-.28	-2.17*
30+ without children	4.51 (71)	4.73 (86)	-.22	-1.76
Family Life Cycle Stage	Dual Wives	House- wives	Difference (DW-HW)	t
Think of divorce (Quality of Life)				
Under 30 without children	4.63 (32)	4.36 (11)	.27	1.02
Preschool children	3.87 (53)	4.40 (156)	-.53	-3.48**
School age children	4.26 (101)	4.58 (107)	-.32	-2.55*
30+ without children	4.52 (71)	4.55 (86)	-.03	-.19

100

WIVES' EMPLOYMENT STATUS AND MARITAL ADJUSTMENT: YET ANOTHER LOOK

Table 2--(continued)

	Marital happiness (Omnibus)			
Under 30 without children	3.22 (23)	3.42 (12)	-.20	-.60
Preschool children	2.72 (46)	3.07 (84)	-.35	-2.37*
School age children	2.82 (83)	2.67 (69)	.15	1.15
30+ without children	2.85 (40)	2.87 (67)	-.02	-.10

*p < .05.
**p < .01.

control variables: family life cycle and education. The tables omit comparisons among husbands on all measures of adjustment and comparisons among wives on the specific measures since these comparisons generated only a few, scattered significant differences.

As regards the two global measures involving marital evaluations, neither of which produces a significant difference between dual wives and housewives at the zero-order level, dual wives register significantly lower marital happiness than housewives among mothers

Table 3

Mean Scores on Global Measures of Marital Adjustment
for Wives, by Wives' Employment Status and Education

Level of Education	Dual Wives	House- wives	Difference (DW-HW)	t
Marital satisfaction (Quality of Life)				
Less than high school diploma	5.80 (61)	6.30 (121)	-.50	-2.34*
High school diploma	6.16 (125)	6.26 (171)	-.10	-.72
Some college	6.00 (42)	6.06 (46)	-.06	-.25
College degree+	6.28 (29)	5.91 (22)	.37	1.35

GRAHAM L. STAINES, *ET AL.*

Table 3—(continued)

Wish married another (Quality of Life)			
Less than high school diploma	4.25 (61)	4.70 (121)	-.45	-3.14**
High school diploma	4.36 (125)	4.55 (171)	-.19	-1.86
Some college	4.14 (42)	4.30 (46)	-.16	-.72
College degree+	4.48 (29)	4.64 (22)	-.16	-.63

Level of Education	Dual Wives	House- wives	Difference (DW-HW)	t
Think of divorce (Quality of Life)				
Less than high school diploma	4.08 (61)	4.55 (121)	-.47	-3.24**
High school diploma	4.40 (125)	4.51 (171)	-.11	-1.07
Some college	4.31 (42)	4.17 (46)	.14	.58
College degree+	4.31 (29)	4.46 (22)	-.15	-.68

Marital happiness (Omnibus)			
Less than high school diploma	2.60 (52)	2.81 (79)	-.21	-1.43
High school diploma	2.91 (91)	2.94 (111)	-.03	-.21
Some college	2.96 (26)	3.03 (32)	-.07	-.30
College degree+	3.08 (25)	3.00 (10)	.08	.28

*$\underline{p}$ < .05.
**$\underline{p}$ < .01.

of preschool children but not among wives in any other stage of the family life cycle (Table 2). Marital satisfaction, in comparison, elicits no significant differences between the two groups of wives for any stage of the life cycle. The pattern changes somewhat for the two global measures concerning marital choices, both of which display significant differences among wives in the total sample. For *wish married another* and *think of divorce,* dual wives report significantly poorer marital adjustment than housewives in the family life-cycle stages with preschool and with school age children, but not in the other two categories.

The results on marital adjustment are presented by level of education in Table 3. On the two global evaluative measures, dual wives score significantly lower on marital satisfaction than housewives among wives with less than a high school diploma but not among wives within any other educational category. Yet no differences emerge in marital happiness between the two groups of wives in any of the four educational categories. The two global measures concerning marital choice (*wish married another* and *think of divorce*) demonstrate significantly lower scores for dual wives than housewives, again within the lowest educational category and no other.

As in the zero-order analyses, the results of these first-order analyses on education differ from those reported by Campbell et al. (1976; also Campbell, 1976). Campbell et al. (1976) presented data concerning only college graduates, again comparing employed wives and housewives using percentage rather than mean differences. They concluded that " . . . it is the highly educated housewife who does not have an outside job whose marriage seems most likely to be beset by disagreements, lack of understanding and companionship, doubts and dissatisfactions" (p. 427). Yet they expressed puzzlement that responses on the item that mentioned thinking about a divorce did not conform to this pattern favoring educated employed wives. As was true of the zero-order comparisons Campbell et al. (1976) did not report significance tests for individual items. Nevertheless, they commented more generally that "it is unlikely that these differences are entirely a matter of chance" (p. 427). The differences between the present results on wives with a college degree and those of Campbell et al. (1976) appear to derive from differences in statistical procedure and group definition. One item in particular illustrates how different statistics can lead to different results. On the question about wishing to have married someone else, the responses of college graduate employed wives tended to fall in the extreme categories at the ends of the scale. Hence, among wives with a college degree, those employed reported more frequently than housewives that they had "never" wished they had married someone else [Campbell et al.'s (1976) result]; yet, simultaneously, they exhibited a higher *average* frequency of wishing they had married someone else (the present result in Table 3).

Not shown here are the results divided by occupational prestige of husband's job, an alternative to respondent's education as a socioeconomic index. The results for these two alternative controls are broadly similar, that is, significant differences favoring housewives over dual wives among lower socioeconomic segments of the samples for three measures only (*marital satisfaction, wish married other,* and *think of divorce*). Yet the comparisons by levels of education address previous findings in the literature more directly and prove more amenable to testing certain theoretical interpretations of the significant differences obtained.

Review and Interpretation of Zero-order and First-order Differences

The data in Tables 1–3 on the effects of wives' employment on marital adjustment uncover a limited set of significant differences for wives but none for husbands. Dual wives score lower than housewives on marital adjustment for the following samples and measures: total sample (*wish married another* and *think of divorce*); mothers of preschool children (*marital happiness, wish married another,* and *think of divorce*); mothers of school-age children (*wish married another* and *think of divorce*); and wives with less education than a high school diploma (*marital satisfaction, wish married another,* and *think of divorce*).

The observed zero-order and first-order differences between dual wives and housewives provide enough evidence to eliminate a number of possible explanations of the lower marital adjustment reported by dual wives. One hypothesis, for example, is that no real difference in marital adjustment exists between dual wives and housewives, but that dual wives are simply more willing to report marital difficulties, perhaps because they are not so totally invested in the marital role that admission of marital problems would be devastating. This hypothesis fails, however, because it implies the existence of consistent mean differences at least across measures of adjustment and possibly across subsamples as well, whereas the observed pattern of results is quite differentiated and specific as to measures and subgroups.

According to another hypothesis, dual wives exhibit lower marital adjustment because their employment and its resulting income disrupts traditional patterns of male dominated authority and decision-making in the family, particularly on financial matters. The hypothesis predicts lower adjustment among dual wives than housewives on the specific item concerning financial disagreements. No such difference appears whatsoever at the zero- or first-order levels. Further, this hypothesis logically implies that dual husbands should score lower than sole breadwinners on marital adjustment generally, and particularly on the item about financial disagreements. As these expected differences are likewise not evident at the zero- or first-order levels, the hypothesis may be rejected.

Differences between dual wives and housewives on demographic variables that are potentially associated with marital adjustment may explain the lower adjustment of dual wives. In the analyses described above, controls on two such variables, family life cycle and education, do not eliminate the significant differences in adjustment found at the zero-order level. Instead, the controls locate the differences in predominantly one stage of the family life cycle (preschool children) and one level of education (less than a high school diploma). Thus, although family life cycle and education are related to the mean differences in marital adjustment, the relationships do not take the simplistic forms suggested by the hypothesis concerning pre-existing differences.

Second-Order Differences Among Mothers of Preschool Children

This section and the one following further investigate possible reasons for the decrement in the marital adjustment of dual wives relative to housewives in two demographic subgroups: mothers of preschool children and wives with less than a high school diploma.

Second-order differences permit tests of two general interpretations of the differences in adjustment between dual wives and housewives. First, dual wives may show lower adjustment because they experience greater role load than housewives. That is, the combined work and family responsibilities of dual wives exceed the family responsibilities of housewives, and such excessive role load (or overload) impairs marital adjustment. The impact of role load on differences in marital adjustment may apply to mothers of preschool children in particular because their role load from parental responsibilities is already considerable, making them and their marriages especially vulnerable to any addition.

To test this interpretation, measures of role load were introduced as controls, and dual wives and housewives with preschool children were compared on marital adjustment within levels of role load. If role load accounts for the mean differences in marital adjustment between dual wives and housewives, these differences should disappear at all levels of the control variables.

Table 4 presents the comparisons relevant to the hypothesis concerning role load, using two different, indirect measures of wives' role load. For the Omnibus Survey, high wives' role load may be inferred when wives indicate they want their husbands to do more child care or housework. In the Quality of Life Survey, wives' reports of feeling "rushed" indicate their level of role load.

As Table 4 demonstrates consistently, controlling for role load does not eliminate the differences in marital adjustment between dual wives and housewives who have preschool children. When role load is low, the differences between the adjustment of dual wives and housewives diminish, yet among wives classified as high on role load, dual wives continue to register significantly lower marital adjustment than housewives. Thus, controlling for level of wife's role load, at least as inferred from the two control measures available here, eliminates some of the significant differences among wives with low but not with high role load.

While failing to support the notion that differences in wives' role load account for dual wives' decrement in marital adjustment among mothers of preschool children, the results in Table 4 do demonstrate that role load moderates the relationship between wives' employment status and marital adjustment in this family life-cycle stage. High role load among wives exacerbates the apparent negative effect of their employment on marital adjustment, whereas low role load minimizes it. Further, in each of the comparisons shown in Table 4, dual wives score significantly lower on marital adjustment in the high than in the low load category. Hence, although level of role load does not explain the differential adjustment of dual wives and housewives who have preschool children, high role load does reduce the adjustment of dual wives.

Aside from issues of role load, the differential marital adjustment of dual wives and housewives among mothers of preschool children may also be investigated in terms of each wife's attitude toward her present role (employment for dual wives, homemaking and housework for housewives) and each husband's attitude toward his wife's present role. It may be plausibly argued that among mothers of preschool children, dual wives are particularly likely to hold ambivalent or negative attitudes toward being employed. Further, husbands of

WIVES' EMPLOYMENT STATUS AND MARITAL ADJUSTMENT: YET ANOTHER LOOK

Table 4

Mean Scores on Global Measures of Marital Adjustment
for Mothers of Preschool Children,
by Wives' Employment Status and Wives' Role Load

Control Variable	Dual Wives	House- wives	Difference (DW-HW)	t
Marital happiness (Omnibus)				
Want more help from husbands				
Yes	2.31^a (26)	2.97 (37)	-.66	-3.19**
No	3.26 (19)	3.15 (46)	.11	.56
Wish married another (Quality of Life)				
Feel rushed				
Always	3.50^a (20)	4.37 (38)	-.87	-3.09**
Sometimes or Almost Never	4.09 (33)	4.52 (118)	-.43	-2.41*
Think of divorce (Quality of Life)				
Feel rushed				
Always	3.40^a (20)	4.21 (38)	-.81	-2.72**
Sometimes or Almost Never	4.15 (33)	4.46 (118)	-.31	-1.77

[a]The difference between high and low role load groups within dual
wives is significant for each of these three comparisons: $t(43)=4.13$,
$p < 0.01$; $t(51)=2.07$, $p < 0.05$; $t(51)=2.65$, $p < 0.05$.

*$p < .05$.
**$p < .01$.

dual wives may be especially likely to disapprove of their wives' employment when preschool children are present in their families. Thus, in theory, controlling for wives' and husbands' attitudes toward wives' present roles might eliminate the differences in adjustment between dual wives and housewives among mothers of preschool children.

Relevant to this hypothesis about attitudes toward wives' roles, Table 5 compares dual wives and housewives, controlling in turn for wives' role commitment, wives' role satisfaction, and husbands' attitudes (as reported by wives) toward their wives' present roles. As noted in the Method section, parallel measures for dual wives and housewives of commitment to present role and satisfaction with present role are available in the Quality of Life Survey; and an item in the Omnibus Survey asking wives to report their husbands' attitudes toward their holding a paid job may be interpreted, by appropriate scoring, as indicating the favorability of husbands' attitudes toward their wives' current roles, whether their wives be employed or homemakers.

Table 5

Mean Scores on Global Measures of Marital Adjustment
for Mothers of Preschool Children,
by Wives' Employment Status and Attitudes to Wives' Current Roles

Control Variables	Dual Wives	House- wives	Difference (DW–HW)	t
Wish married another (Quality of Life)				
Wives' Role Commitment				
High	3.83 (30)	4.53 (122)	-.70	-3.93**
Low	3.91 (23)	4.37 (30)	-.46	-1.58
Think of divorce (Quality of Life)				
Wives' Role Commitment				
High	3.97 (30)	4.43 (122)	-.46	-2.49*
Low	3.74 (23)	4.43 (30)	-.69	-2.44*

WIVES' EMPLOYMENT STATUS AND MARITAL ADJUSTMENT: YET ANOTHER LOOK

Table 5--(continued)

Wish married another (Quality of Life)				
Wives' Role Satisfaction				
High	3.86 (29)	4.60 (111)	-.74	-4.00**
Low	3.88 (24)	4.18 (44)	-.30	-1.16

Control Variables	Dual Wives	House- wives	Difference (DW-HW)	t
Think of divorce (Quality of Life)				
Wives' Role Satisfaction				
High	3.79 (29)	4.51 (111)	-.72	-3.93**
Low	3.96 (24)	4.11 (44)	-.15	-.57

Marital happiness (Omnibus)				
Husbands' Attitudes to Wives' Present Roles[a]				
Approving	2.55 (20)	3.07 (45)	-.52	-2.31*
Neutral	2.67 (6)	3.25 (16)	-.58	-1.70
Disapproving	2.83 (6)	2.91 (21)	-.08	-.19

[a]Dual wives with preschool children and employed fewer than 20 hours per week were excluded from this control analysis, since the item on which this variable was based specified husband's attitude toward the respondent's being employed at least half-time.

*$\underline{p} < .05$.

**$\underline{p} < .01$.

Contrary to expectation, among mothers of preschool children, controlling for these measures of wives' and husbands' attitudes toward wives' current roles does not eliminate the differences in marital adjustment attributable to wives' employment status. In all cases, the differences between the adjustment of dual wives and housewives remain significant among wives reporting favorable attitudes toward their role, either on their own or their husbands' part. Thus, among mothers of preschool children, possible differences in wives' or husbands' attitudes toward wives' present roles do not account for the significant decrement in marital adjustment of dual wives relative to housewives. But, as in the preceding analyses concerning wives' role load, attitudes toward wives' present roles moderate the effects of wives' employment on marital adjustment.

In addition, Table 5 permits a partial test of a variant hypothesis concerning the relationship between wives' role commitment and marital adjustment. Though not central to the line of analysis pursued here, this hypothesis merits brief consideration. Dual wives may score low on marital adjustment because wives who are disenchanted with their marriages enter the labor force and become highly committed to the work role. This hypothesis implies a negative association among dual wives between commitment to present role (i.e., employment) and marital adjustment for the preschool category. Yet Table 5 demonstrates virtually no association between work commitment and marital adjustment among employed mothers of preschool children.

Second-order Differences Among Wives With Less Than a High School Diploma

The two general explanations just considered for the decrement in the marital adjustment of dual wives relative to housewives among mothers of preschool children may now be applied to dual wives' decrement in marital adjustment among women with less than a high school diploma.

There are several ways in which wives' and husbands' attitudes to wives' present roles might account for dual wives' decrement in marital adjustment among less educated wives. First, less educated dual wives may take paid employment primarily because of their families' economic needs rather than their own desires to be employed, in effect being forced into the labor market for economic reasons. Wives' employment under such adverse circumstances may be particularly likely to lead to difficulties in marital adjustment. If this interpretation is correct, differences between dual wives and housewives should disappear when commitment to present role, whether dual wife or housewife, is controlled. Hence, the critical control concerns whether wives would choose to continue in their present roles even if they did not have to (for dual wives, if they had enough money to live comfortably; for housewives, if they had someone to take care of things at home).

A related interpretation involves the job experiences of dual wives with less than a high school diploma. Such wives typically face a job market that offers few attractive occupational possibilities, and they frequently work at relatively unsatisfying jobs. Thus, wives' employment may lead to a decrement in marital adjustment specifically among wives with less than a high school diploma because their jobs tend to be particularly unsatisfying. If this interpretation holds true, differences in marital adjustment among least educated wives should be reduced or eliminated when a control is imposed on wives' satisfaction with their present roles, that is, job satisfaction for dual wives and satisfaction with homemaking and housework for housewives.

Table 6 compares the marital adjustment of dual wives and housewives with less than a high school diploma, controlling first for role commitment and then for role satisfaction. For all three measures of marital adjustment, among wives high in role commitment, dual wives' decrement in marital adjustment remains significant. For wives low in role commitment, the differences between dual wives' and housewives' adjustment, although still large, are not statistically significant. The control on role satisfaction slightly increases dual wives' decrement in marital adjustment within the low satisfaction category, such that two of the differences in adjustment achieve significance among wives with low education. The same control slightly lowers the decrement in the high satisfaction category, and none of these differences attains significance.

A further argument about the differential adjustment of dual wives and housewives refers to the attitudes of husbands toward their wives' present roles. Less educated wives tend to marry less educated husbands who may hold traditional, hence disapproving, attitudes toward the employment of their wives. The absence of a difference in the marital happiness of less educated dual wives and housewives prevents a full test of the hypothesis about husbands' attitudes because there is no significant mean difference for the control variable to reduce. Yet it remains possible to test the hypothesis partially by determining whether the distributions on the control variable are compatible with its predictions. According to data not shown in Table

6, eight out of 48 (or 17%) of the dual wives who work at least half
time report that their husbands disapprove of their working, whereas
14 housewives out of 77 (or 18%) suggest indirectly that their husbands disapprove of their staying home. The near identity of these
distributions appears to eliminate the hypothesis that the difference in
the marital adjustment of less educated dual wives and housewives
stems from husbands' attitudes to their wives' present roles.
Although not critical to the argument here, it remains interesting

Table 6

Mean Scores on Global Measures of Marital Adjustment
for Wives with Less Than a High School Diploma,
by Wives' Employment Status and Attitudes to Wives' Current Roles
(Quality of Life Survey)

Control Variables	Dual Wives	House- wives	Difference (DW-HW)	t
Marital satisfaction				
Wives' Role Commitment				
High	5.83 (29)	6.37 (98)	-.54	-1.99*
Low	5.84 (31)	6.14 (21)	-.30	-.73
Wish married another				
Wives' Role Commitment				
High	4.24 (29)	4.71 (98)	-.47	-2.54*
Low	4.23 (31)	4.62 (21)	-.39	-1.31
Think of divorce				
Wives' Role Commitment				
High	4.14 (29)	4.54 (98)	-.40	-2.20*
Low	4.10 (31)	4.67 (21)	-.57	-1.92

WIVES' EMPLOYMENT STATUS AND MARITAL ADJUSTMENT: YET ANOTHER LOOK

Table 6--(continued)

Control Variables	Dual Wives	House- wives	Difference (DW-HW)	t
Marital satisfaction				
Wives' Role Satisfaction				
High	6.11 (26)	6.45 (67)	-.34	-1.07
Low	5.57 (35)	6.13 (53)	-.56	-1.93
Wish married another				
Wives' Role Satisfaction				
High	4.50 (26)	4.78 (67)	-.28	-1.36
Low	4.06 (35)	4.60 (53)	-.54	-2.59*
Think of divorce				
Wives' Role Satisfaction				
High	4.19 (26)	4.58 (67)	-.39	-1.84
Low	4.00 (35)	4.53 (53)	-.53	-2.56*

*$\underline{p}$ < .05.

to ask whether a control on husbands' attitudes to their wives' present roles (not shown in Table 6) uncovers any significant differences in marital happiness between dual wives and housewives that are not present among all wives with less than a high school diploma. According to the relevant t tests, the answer is negative.

An overview of the two analyses presented in Table 6 indicates that differences in neither wives' role commitment nor wives' role satisfaction account for the differences in marital adjustment between less educated dual wives and housewives, in that significant differences between dual wives and housewives persist even after these variables have been controlled. In both control analyses, significant differences generally remain within one level of the control but not the other. This pattern may suggest that the control variable acts as a moderator of the effects of wives' employment on marital adjustment rather than simply as a confounding third variable that must be controlled for. It should be noted, though, that the differences in the dual wives' decrement in marital adjustment between the high and low categories of each control variable are not great. It should likewise be observed that the apparent moderating effects of wives' role commitment and role satisfaction are not consistent with each other. That is, dual wives' decrement in marital adjustment relative to housewives' appears exacerbated by high role commitment but, to a greater extent, by low role satisfaction.

Table 6 also allows a partial test of the variant hypothesis concerning the relationship between wives' role commitment and marital adjustment. The hypothesis was cited earlier in connection with mothers of preschool children but it may also be tested for wives with less than a high school diploma. As noted earlier, the hypothesis implies that among dual wives high work commitment is associated with low marital adjustment. Like Table 5, Table 6 indicates virtually no differences in marital adjustment between dual wives high and low on work-role commitment.

The significant differences between dual wives' and housewives' marital adjustment among wives with less than a high school education may also be considered in light of wives' role load. An argument can be made that role load explains the difference in adjustment between dual wives and housewives in the low education category. Less educated dual wives may hold traditional views about the division of domestic labor and may not feel entitled to ask or to expect their husbands to help them with domestic tasks. Few of them, presumably, can afford paid domestic help. Thus, controlling for wives' role load may diminish the differences in marital adjustment between dual wives and housewives.

The data in Table 7 do not support this prediction. A significant difference in marital adjustment remains among wives low in role load. Thus, once again, a control variable acts as a moderator of the effect of wives' employment on marital adjustment, rather than as a confounding factor that, when controlled for, eliminates the negative effects of wives' employment.

Though not presented in Table 7, the Omnibus data permit one

WIVES' EMPLOYMENT STATUS AND MARITAL ADJUSTMENT: YET ANOTHER LOOK

Table 7

Mean Scores on Global Measures of Marital Adjustment
for Wives with Less Than a High School Diploma,
by Wives' Employment Status and Wives' Role Load (Quality of Life)

Control Variable	Dual Wives	House- wives	Difference (DW-HW)	t
Marital satisfaction				
Feel Rushed				
Always	5.41 (17)	5.26 (23)	.15	.27
Sometimes or Almost Never	5.96 (44)	6.54 (98)	-.58	-2.91**
Wish married another				
Feel Rushed				
Always	4.41 (17)	4.57 (23)	-.16	-.43
Sometimes or Almost Never	4.18 (44)	4.74 (98)	-.56	-3.51**
Think of divorce				
Feel Rushed				
Always	3.88 (17)	4.09 (23)	-.21	-.56
Sometimes or Almost Never	4.16 (44)	4.66 (98)	-.50	-3.33**

*$\underline{p} < .01$.

further but only partial test of the role-load hypothesis as applied to wives with limited education. The role-load measure concerning wives' desire for more help from their husbands permits a check on the predicted distributions of cases. Seventeen dual wives out of 33 (or 52%) comment that they would like more help from their husbands in either childcare or housework (or both), whereas 18 of 46 housewives (or 39%) express a desire for more husband help. These proportions are clearly compatible with the interpretation that dual wives in the low education group are overloaded more than housewives, but a complete test using desire for more husband help as a control variable is ruled out by the absence of a significant difference on marital happiness between dual wives and housewives in the low education category. (Less educated dual wives and housewives may nonetheless be compared on marital happiness within levels of the control on wanting more husband help. Again, the *t* tests reveal no significant differences at this second-order level.)

SUMMARY AND CONCLUSIONS

To summarize the preceding results, dual wives display significantly lower marital adjustment than housewives on two of four global measures: wishing one had married someone else, and having thought about getting a divorce. When controls for family life-cycle stage and level of education are introduced, the decrement in the marital adjustment of dual wives relative to housewives is shown to be restricted as regards life cycle primarily to mothers of preschool children, and as regards education to wives with less than a high school diploma. For each of these demographic subgroups, significant differences also emerge on an additional global measure of marital adjustment: marital happiness for mothers of preschool children, and marital satisfaction for wives with less than a high school diploma. In addition, only a few, scattered significant differences were found between dual wives and housewives on four more specific measures of marital adjustment, and between sole breadwinning and dual husbands on any of the dependent measures.

The results in this paper square with most of the comparable findings in previous literature. At the zero-order level, the pattern of results obtained resembles the pattern reported earlier for 13 studies that included comparisons between dual wives and housewives. In this study, as in the previous literature, dual wives score significantly lower in marital adjustment than housewives in only a few comparisons, nonsignificantly lower than housewives in others, and differ hardly at all from housewives in still others. There is also precedent in previous literature for the present pattern of zero-order results concerning overall evaluations of marriage (marital satisfaction and marital happiness) as compared to other global measures of marital adjustment. In Nye's (1959) study of mothers from white, nonfarm families in three Washington towns, employed wives reported thoughts of divorce significantly more often than housewives but did not report significantly lower marital satisfaction or happiness. The present data also accord with previous literature concerning which levels of education sharpen or weaken the differences between the adjustment of dual wives and housewives. The tendency in the recent literature toward a greater decrement of dual wives' adjustment relative to housewives among less rather than more educated women is replicated quite clearly in the present analyses.

Interpretation of the present findings requires a careful sifting of methodological issues. In particular, a close examination is needed of the dependent measures of marital adjustment and the secondary controls used to test alternative explanations of significant group differences on adjustment. As regards the dependent measures, Ny's (1959) findings, taken in conjunction with those obtained here, suggest the importance of distinguishing positive from negative measures of marital adjustment. Positive measures tap positive affect (as in marital happiness) or positive assessments (as in marital satisfaction). Negative measures tap marital conflict and thoughts of separation, alternative spouses, and divorce. The data in Nye's (1959) study and the zero-order comparisons in the present one indicate that employment can increase wives' negative sentiments and discontent about their marriages without reducing positive satisfaction and happiness. Only in the two sample subgroups where wives' employment has the strongest effects on marriage does it significantly reduce wives' marital satisfaction or happiness as well.

Also deserving methodological comment in the present study are the differences between the findings obtained for global vs. specific measures of adjustment. Global measures prove sensitive to the effects of wives' employment in the overall samples and in certain demographic subgroups; the specific measures used here do not. It may be that specific measures are inherently less sensitive to the effects of wives' employment than global ones. Alternatively, the specific measures available here may simply not have included the most relevant ones.

As to the control variables employed in the second-order comparisons, the measures tapping wives' role load appear inferior to those tapping wives' and husbands' attitudes to wives' present roles. Both measures of wives' role load (wives' wishes for more domestic help from their husbands, and frequency of feeling rushed) are indirect, in that they assess wives' role load by recording its presumed subjective consequences for wives. Nonetheless, the indirectness of the measures of load can scarcely be blamed for the lack of support for the role-load hypothesis as applied to mothers of preschool children. To the extent that the measures of load are indirect, hence poor estimates of real load, they would nullify differences between high and low load categories. Yet, such differences appear consistently within and across both datasets.

The first of the two measures of role load, wives' wishes for more domestic help from their husbands, has a further defect. Many wives who experience high load may not express a wish for their husbands to help more, because of traditional beliefs that only women should perform child care and housework. Thus, although all wives in the high-load category on this measure experience high load, some of those in the low-load category may actually encounter high-role load but fail to report a desire for more husband help. But this possible defect in the measure cannot account for the present finding that dual wives register significantly lower marital adjustment than housewives in the high-load condition. If the hypothesis concerning role load is accurate, differences in marital adjustment between the two groups of wives should disappear when role load is controlled, i.e., within levels of role load. Since the measure of role load is unproblematic for the high-load category, it should yield no significant mean differences on marital adjustment. Significant differences nonetheless appear.

As regards the hypotheses receiving major attention here, excessive role load does not account for the lower adjustment of dual wives among mothers of preschool children. Controls on three measures of role load do not eliminate the significant effects of wives' employment status. Thus, the notion of role load as an intervening mechanism linking wives' employment status and marital adjustment proves unsound. Instead, role load moderates the relationship between employment status and adjustment in an entirely plausible fashion. Except for one comparison, among the relevant measures of load in both datasets, the negative impact of employment on dual wives' adjustment relative to housewives is significant among and only among those with high load. That is, only among wives who feel overburdened by their responsibilities do those who work report lower adjustment in their marriages.

Still concerned with the decrement in dual wives' adjustment among mothers of preschool children, wives' and husbands' attitudes toward wives' present roles display only limited explanatory power. Controls on attitudes to wives' present roles again do not eliminate the differences between the two groups of wives. These attitudes instead have a moderating effect, but one difficult to interpret: With only one exception among the relevant comparisons, dual wives' decrement in marital adjustment is significant among and only among wives reporting *positive* scores on the various measures of attitudes toward their present roles. In the control on husbands' attitudes, however, the small number of cases of dual wives reporting neutral or disapproving attitudes in their husbands substantially reduces the utility of this particular control.

Differences in wives' and husbands' attitudes to wives' present roles promise a plausible explanation for the decrement in the marital adjustment of dual wives among the group without a high school diploma. Yet, controlling for wives' attitudes to their present roles does not eliminate the mean differences. Dual wives' decrement in marital adjustment consistently remains significant in the high role-commitment group. In one of these comparisons, however, the mean difference in marital adjustment is actually greater in absolute terms, though not significant, in the low role-commitment group. Dual wives' decrement in marital adjustment proves to be significant in the low-satisfaction group in two out of three comparisons. Possible moderating effects are difficult to interpret here, because the patterns within each of these two second-order control analyses are somewhat less consistent than in the preceding analyses. Further complicating interpretation, the results of these two control analyses are not consistent with each other; that is, a significant difference between dual wives and housewives tends to remain when wives have *high* role commitment but also when they have *low* role satisfaction. A complete test was not possible of the hypothesis concerning husbands' attitudes toward wives' present roles, but the distributional pattern alone demonstrates that dual wives are no more or less likely than housewives to report that their husbands disapprove of their present roles.

Role load, an alternative causal explanation of the marital adjustment differences in the low-education category, moderates rather than accounts for the effects of wives' employment on adjustment. That is, controlling for role load does not eliminate all mean differences. Rather, the differences between dual wives and housewives remain substantial and significant for the low: but not the high-load category. This moderating effect is a curious one: Wives' employment would plausibly be expected to have a stronger negative effect on marital adjustment in the high rather than in the low role-load category. Distributional tests are, however, consistent with the role-load hypothesis for the items on wanting more husband help at home, since more dual wives than housewives express a desire for additional husband help.

To recapitulate, the findings for the specific hypotheses tested among mothers of preschool children and wives with less than a high school diploma are broadly negative. In no instance do the major causal mechanisms, wives' role load and wives' and husbands' attitudes toward wives' present roles, account for the decrement in the marital adjustment of dual wives. It is possible that better measures of secondary controls, especially wives' role load, would produce fewer negative results. It is also possible that only a radically different set of hypotheses would abolish the negative pattern. If so, datasets other than the present two will probably be needed.

The analyses do, however, uncover one plausible and relatively consistent moderating effect that emerges clearly for the relevant measures of load and adjustment in both datasets: Among mothers of preschool children, a significant relationship between wives' employment and adjustment exists primarily among those high in role load. Two other relatively consistent moderating effects occur, but these are counterintuitive: Among mothers of preschool children, dual wives' significant decrement in marital adjustment appears primarily among those reporting *positive* scores on the attitudinal variables; and among wives with less than a high school diploma, the decrement occurs significantly only among those *low* in role load. Finally, the moderating effects of wives' role commitment and role satisfaction among less educated wives follow no consistent pattern. None of these counterintuitive or inconsistent moderating effects, however, could be adequately tested in the two present datasets. Further research should pursue these paradoxical moderating effects, and, if they are successfully replicated, research should investigate their dynamics.

REFERENCES

Axelson, L. J. The marital adjustment and marital role definitions of husbands of working and nonworking wives. *Marriage and Family Living*, 1963, *25*, 189–195.

Babbie, E. R. *Survey research methods*. Belmont: Wadsworth Publishing, 1973.

Blood, R. O., Jr., & Wolfe, D. M. *Husbands and wives*. Glencoe, Ill.: Free Press, 1960.

Buric, O., & Zecevic, A. Family authority, marital satisfaction, and the social network in Yugoslavia. *Journal of Marriage and the Family*, 1967, *29*, 325–336.

Burke, R. J., & Weir, T. Relationship of wives' employment status to husband, wife, and pair satisfaction and performance. *Journal of Marriage and the Family*, 1976, *38*, 279–287.

Campbell, A., Converse, P. E., & Rodgers, W. L. *The quality of american life: Perceptions, evaluations, and satisfactions*. New York: Russell Sage Foundation, 1976.

WIVES' EMPLOYMENT STATUS AND MARITAL ADJUSTMENT: YET ANOTHER LOOK

Campbell, A. Women at home and at work. In D. McGuigan (Ed.), *New research on women and sex roles*. Ann Arbor, Mich.: Center for Continuing Education of Women, 1976.

Chesser, E. *The sexual, marital, and family relationships of the English woman*. Watford: Hutchinson's Medical Publications, 1956.

Davis, K. B. *Factors in the sex life of twenty-two hundred women*. New York, Harper, 1929.

Feld, S. Feelings of adjustment. In F. I. Nye & L. W. Hoffman (Eds.), *The employed mother in America*. Chicago: Rand McNally, 1963.

Feldman, H. *Development of the husband-wife relationship*. (Research report to the National Institute of Mental Health.) Ithaca: Cornell University, Department of Human Development and Family Studies, 1965.

Fidell, L. *Employment status, role dissatisfaction, and the housewife syndrome*. Unpublished manuscript, 1977a. (Available from Department of Psychology, California State University, Northridge, California 91324.)

Fidell, L. Personal communication, March 18, 1977b.

Fogarty, M. P., Rapoport, R., & Rapoport, R. N. *Sex, career, and family*. London: George Allen & Unwin, 1971.

Gover, D. Socio-economic differential in the relationship between marital adjustment and wife's employment status. *Marriage and Family Living*, 1963, *25*, 452–458.

Gross, R. H., & Arvey, R. D. Marital satisfaction, job satisfaction, and task distribution in the homemaker job. *Journal of Vocational Behavior*, 1977, *11*, 1–13.

Haavio-Mannila, E. Satisfaction with family, work, leisure, and life among men and women. *Human Relations*, 1971, *24*, 585–601.

Hauenstein, L. S. *Attitudes of married women toward work and family* (Reports 1 and 2). Ann Arbor: University of Michigan, Department of Psychology, 1976.

Locke, H. J., & Mackeprang, M. Marital adjustment and the employed wife. *American Journal of Sociology*, 1949, *54*, 536–538.

Michel, A. Comparative data concerning the interaction in French and American families. *Journal of Marriage and the Family*, 1967, *29*, 337–344.

Nye, F. I. Employment status of mothers and marital conflict, permanence, and happiness. *Social Problems*, 1959, *6*, 260–267.

Orden, S. R., & Bradburn, N. M. Working wives and marriage happiness. *American Journal of Sociology*, 1969, *74*, 392–407.

Radloff, L. Sex differences in depression: The effects of occupation and marital status. *Sex Roles*, 1975, *1*, 249–265.

Robinson, J. P., Yerby, J., Feiweger, M., & Somerick, N. Time use as an indicator of sex role territoriality. *Sex Roles*, in press.

Safilios-Rothschild, C. A comparison of power structure and marital satisfaction in urban Greek and French families. *Journal of Marriage and the Family*, 1967, *29*, 345–352.

Safilios-Rothschild, C. The influence of the wife's degree of work commitment upon some aspects of family organization and dynamics. *Journal of Marriage and the Family*, 1970, *32*, 681–691.

Scanzoni, J. H. *Opportunity and the family*. New York: Free Press, 1970.

Tavris, C. A. The unliberated liberals: Attitudes toward the issues of women's liberation (Doctoral dissertation, University of Michigan, 1971). *Dissertation Abstracts International*, 1972, *32*, 6542A (University Microfilms No. 72-15, 013).

Tavris, C. A., & Jayaratne, T. How happy is your marriage? *Redbook*, June 1976, pp. 90–92; 132; 134.